WHAT TO DO WHEN
THE
BILL
COLLECTOR
CALLS!

KNOW YOUR RIGHTS

DAVID L. KELCHER, Jr.

WHAT TO DO WHEN THE BILL COLLECTOR CALLS!

KNOW YOUR RIGHTS

DAVID L. KELCHER, Jr.

P.O. Box 4123, Lancaster, Pennsylvania 17604

To schedule Author appearances write:
Author Appearances, Starburst Promotions, P. O. Box 4123, Lancaster, PA 17604 or call (717) 293-0939.

Credits:

Cover art by Dave Ivey

First Printing, July 1991

ISBN: 0-914984-32-2
Library of Congress Catalog Number 91-65403

Printed in the United States of America

Dedication

To my wife and best friend *Donna*, who has always sacrificed herself for me; my daughter *Amanda*, who put up with me while I wrote this book; my newest addition, *Britney Nicole;* and for so much love from *Francis* and *Leo Klema, Willa* and *George, Sunni* and *Mark Nabors; Robert W. Faid*, who expertly guided me along; and most of all,

OUR LORD AND SAVIOR JESUS CHRIST.

Contents

Introduction   13

Illegal Phone Call   17

Chapter 1 — The Account   25
   Placing The Account With An Agency   26
   Interest Free Account   28
   Furnishing Deceptive Forms   29

Chapter 2 — The Search   33
   Post Office Boxes   34
   Non-Published Numbers   35
   Hours of Calling   36
   Calling At An Inconvienient Time   38
   Time Zones   39
   Time Zone Map   40
   Answering Machines   41
   Phone Number Con Game   42

Chapter 3 — The Contact   43
   First Letter Notification   44
   Disputed Debts   49
   When A Bill Collector First Calls   53
   Third Party Disclosure   55
   Calling You At Work   58
   Hang-Ups   60

Ceasing Communication   61
Key Words   63
They Can't Say What They Won't Do   64
False or Misleading Representations   67
Harassment   71
Vulgar Language Or Name Calling   73

Chapter 4 — The Payment   75
Multiple Debts   76
The Big Lie   77
Payment Arrangements   78
Offer A Settlement   83
Adding Expenses To The Bill   87
It's In The Mail   89
Overnight Delivery   90
Postdated Checks   91
Paid In Full   93
Will a Creditor Sue?   94
A Judgement Against You   98
Purchased Accounts   103
Consumer Credit Counseling Services   104
Credit Cards   106
Bankrupty, A Way Out   112

Chapter 5 — Location Information   117
Credit Application Information   118
Credit Bureau Reports   120
Permissable Purposes Of Consumer Reports   122
Procedure In Case Of Disputed Accuracy   126

Social Security Reports   131
City Directory   132

Chapter 6 — Suing An Agency   133

Incident Report   137
Closing Statement   139

Fair Debt Collection Practices Act   141
History Of The Legislation   142
Nature And Purpose Of The Bill   142
Need For This Legislation   143
Explanation Of The Legislation   145
Obtaining Location Information   146
Prohibited Practices   147
Validation Of Debts   148
Legal Actions By Debt Collectors   148
Furnishing Deceptive Forms   149
Civil Liability   149
Administrative Enforcement   150
Relation To State Law   150
Cost Of This Legislation   151

Summary of the Legislation   153

Individual State Laws   159
Index   185
Sources   189

Preface

Having enjoyed successful years in Debt Collection, which included receiving the COLLECTOR HALL OF FAME AWARD, I realize that the majority of consumers are totally unarmed against Collection Agencies. The ever increasing need for Consumers to be informed of their rights has prompted me to compile this informative book. As a result of my years as a Debt Collector, I believe I can see a clearer picture than the ordinary Consumer: understanding the laws pertaining to Debt Collection, and having *inside* information as to what *really* goes on inside a Collection Agency. EVERYONE has something to gain by reading this book.

Introduction

To many people, *What To Do When The Bill Collector Calls* is a very embarrassing subject and is to be avoided as much as possible. Purchasing a book of this nature could also be an embarrassment. Some people would shy away from the idea of going to a public bookstore and, in front of other customers, picking up a book of this nature. Actually purchasing this type of book is even more intimidating. It is like admitting to everyone that you are in financial trouble. Go ahead, purchase the book. Hide it deep in the bag, and when you get home, tuck it safely under the bed. If you are being harassed by Bill Collectors this will be the most informative book you've ever purchased.

There is much evidence of the abusive, deceptive, and unfair practices of many Debt Collectors. Abusive debt collection practices contribute to personal bankruptcies, marital instability, the loss of jobs, and the invasion of individual privacy. You are not alone if you are having debt problems or are concerned about your present financial situation. Your concern is shared by hundreds of thousands of people. The problem is that there is not enough money available from your income to make full payments to all of your Creditors. Obviously, you are concerned enough about your financial situation to read this book. Heading off the situation before it falls into a Collector's hands is your key to success.

Many people could avoid having their account turned over to a Bill Collector if they recognized the warning signs of getting "in over their head" financially:

1. Paying each month the minimum (or less) amount due on your bills.

2. Fighting in the home over money problems.

3. Not knowing how much you owe.

4. Using savings for daily expenses.

5. Using cash advances from one credit card to pay another credit card or to pay daily expenses.

6. Creditors calling to notify you of a late payment.

7. Making minimum monthly payments to Creditors totaling 20% or more of your take home pay (not including rent or mortgage).

The vast majority of Consumers who obtain credit fully intend to repay their debts. In 1977, government reports revealed that only 4% of the defaulting Debtors intended to cheat their Creditors by willfully refusing to pay their debts. Why then do people stereotype Debtors into the term "Deadbeat?" Ninety-six percent of the people WANT to resolve their financial obligations, but seem to have slipped into an uncontrollable situation which many others borderline today. Some of these are: divorce, catastrophic illness, layoff, mismanagement, inflation, over extension, or the increasing ease of obtaining "instant credit."

There is no need to feel shame if a Bill Collector calls you about a bill. Thousands of people are called every day. You would be surprised to learn how many of these are your own neighbors. Debt Collection by third party Collection Agencies is a substantial business which touches the lives of many Americans. There are more than 6,000 Collection Agencies across the country, each averaging 20 employees. Last year, more than $72.3 billion were turned over to Collection Agencies, which reached millions of Consumers. In the 1970's and before, Debt Collection abuse by third party Collection Agencies was widespread and a serious national problem. The problem is less obvious now, since the Federal Government passed a law in 1977 (which went into effect on the 20th of March, 1978), called the FAIR DEBT COLLECTION PRACTICES ACT. Unfortunately, there are still unscrupulous Bill Collectors who, when given the opportunity, will abuse the Debtor with threats of violence, use of obscene or profane language, telephone calls at unreasonable hours, misrepresentation of CONSUMER RIGHTS, disclosure of the Consumer's personal affairs to friends, neighbors, or an employer, obtaining information about a Consumer through false pretense, impersonating Public Officials and Attorneys, and simulating legal process.

The purpose of the *Fair Debt Collection Practices Act* is to protect Consumers from a host of unfair, harassing, and deceptive Debt Collection practices without imposing unnecessary restrictions on "ethical" Debt Collectors. While unscrupulous Debt Collectors comprise only a small segment of the industry, the suffering and anguish which they regularly inflict is substantial. Why? To make you pay your bills, because they receive a percentage of the money collected.

I believe the primary reason why Debt Collection abuse is so widespread is because of the lack of Consumer education. If the Consumer knows nothing about the laws concerning Debt Collection, then the Collection Agent can "walk all over" the Consumer. How is the Consumer to know that what is happening is illegal? Bills are flooding in, he can't make ends meet, Bill Collectors are calling him at work, and he's afraid he's going to lose his job. The last thing he is worried about is if his RIGHTS are protected, because he doesn't realize he has RIGHTS. This book will help.

Unfortunately, Collection Agencies are a necessary part of our society. Without them, we could expect to pay at least "Double" the current price for anything we buy today. Without Collection Agencies, the economy of the United States would literally collapse and cause economic disaster. So if we *must* live with Collection Agencies in our country, then we *must* know our RIGHTS concerning them, and what to do when they deviate from the law.

RIGHTS: *That which is due anyone by law, a just or legal claim or title. According to law, morality or justice.*

Illegal Phone Call

Collector   "Hi, is this the Smith residence?"

Neighbor   "Yes it is. May I help you?"

Collector   "Yes, my name is Mike, and I'm trying to get in touch with your next door neighbor, Mrs. Jones. I thought that if I called you, then you might be able to get a message to her for me."

So far so good, The Collector starts out in a professional manner, and does nothing to cause concern to the neighbor.

Neighbor   "Well I don't know, I don't . . . ."

Collector   "I just want to leave a message. It's an EMERGENCY!"

He didn't last very long before he broke the law. Stating that this matter is an "EMERGENCY" is a lie and cannot be said. He may say that it is "URGENT" or if an "IMPORTANT" personal business matter.

Neighbor   "Oh, what's the emergency? Did someone die? Is someone sick?"

Collector   "Don't worry about it. I have to talk to
             her now, but she has a non-published
             number. Just tell me her number or where
             she works. I'll call her there."

The 3rd party (neighbor) is now being abused
by being told "Don't worry about it." He is
conveying to her that it is none of her business,
when in fact he is now *making* it her business. She
is the one doing the favor by taking the message
to the consumer. He seems to be demanding that
she give him information.

Neighbor   "Well, I don't know. She doesn't want her
            number given out to just anyone."

Collector   "I'm not just anybody. I'm uh—uh a friend,
            and she's expecting my call."

Neighbor   "Where do you know her from, and what's
            the emergency?"

Collector   "Look lady, just give me the number, and
            mind your own business. I just know her.
            OK?"

A Bill Collector may not "LIE," as he has done
numerous times already. He is *not* her friend, he
does *not* know her, and she is *not* necessarily
expecting his call. If she were, she would have made
sure the Collector had her phone number to begin
with.

Neighbor   "Where did you get my number, and how
            did you know my name?"

Collector   "Button your lip lady and give me her number. This doesn't concern you."

This *does* concern her now. She's concerned about where he obtained her number and how he knew her name. He should have told her, he used the City Directory which gave the street name and who lives on that street. Her number was chosen by the collector because she lives next door. Telling her to "button her lip" is out and out harassment and abuse. This is uncalled for and is not professional.

Neighbor   "Who are you REALLY? This whole thing seems a little fishy to me. I'm calling the police."

Collector   (click)—He hangs up on her.

This collector has not only harassed this neighbor, but has really put fear into her. As far as she's concerned, this is a crazy person, and he knows her phone number. She did the right thing by saying she'll call the police. Not only was the collector rude, but he hung up on her. He probably realized the neighbor knew that his tactics were illegal, and he wasn't about to stick around any longer.
He finally obtains her work number from another neighbor.

Collector   (calling her work number) "Hi, Mrs. Jones please."

Employee   "May I ask whose calling?"

Collector   "Mike, and hurry it up!"

Employee   "She can't accept personal phone calls. Would you like to leave your name and number? I can have her call you back when she gets home tonight."

Collector   "No! I need to speak to her NOW. It's an EMERGENCY!"

Obviously, this collector likes the work "EMERGENCY," which is still against the law. Already he is harassing the telephone receptionist. He was told Mary Jones cannot accept personal phone calls. He should have left it at that. If no calls are allowed at work, then he may *not* call her on the job. The best he is allowed to do by law is to attempt to leave a message. He is not to *demand* to speak to her. If this ever happens, make sure the receptionist gets his name and phone number. Next, call the collector back and ask for his supervisor. His supervisor would be very interested in hearing what this collector is up to.

Employee   "Please hold."

Collector   "Hi, is this Mary Jones?"

Consumer   "Yes, this is she.
             There's an EMERGENCY?
             What's wrong? Please don't say . . . ."

Already the Consumer is terrified when she heard this is an EMERGENCY call. I'm sure she thought the worst. Can you see why the term EMERGENCY may not be used? He deceived the Consumer into coming to the phone.

Collector   "Mrs. Jones if you just shut up for a second, I'll tell you. I'm calling about your credit card with (blank). You're past due, and my client wants their money NOW. Pay it, or pay the consequences."

When a collector calls, he is required by law to first state his name, company name, and who the creditor is. He did not do this. He immediately demanded the money. He also threatened her by saying she would "pay the consequences." What consequences? This sounds like an *open threat* that leaves the consumer to imagine what those consequences might be. He did not state what those consequences might be. He is relying on the fact that her imagination will run away with her. Telling a debtor to "shut up" is definitely not professional.

Consumer   "Look, you have no right to . . . ."

Collector   "Lady, I'm processing your PAPERWORK towards LITIGATION. Either pay your bill now or get an Attorney. Take your pick."

He is leaving her with the impression that she is being sued, when in fact she is not. He is just *processing* it *towards* LITIGATION. In the heat of the conversation, she only heard LITIGATION and ATTORNEY. Consumers usually jump to conclusions when they hear the words LITIGATION and ATTORNEY.

Consumer   "Why don't you call me at home. I'll get fired for personal calls."

Collector   "Your number is non-published. ALL you DEADBEAT'S numbers are non-published."

The consumer was down-graded by being called a DEADBEAT. He is not allowed name calling or swearing. It is against the law. Her place of employment does not allow personal calls, yet the Bill Collector bullied his way through people to get to her.

Consumer   "Look, I can pay $25 per month, but there is no way I can pay $500 all at one time. Anyway, stop calling me at work. I have RIGHTS too you know."

Collector   "Lady, you have no RIGHTS. You're nothing but a lousy debtor. As for your $25 per month offer, HA! You owe $500, and I want it NOW."

Obviously the lady does not know that she can make him stop calling her at work (as you will see later in this book). If she knew how to negotiate, she could have pushed for the $25 per month, and probably gotten her way. The collector did not let her know she has rights, when in fact, he blatantly told her that she has no rights at all. Again, he has insulted her by calling her a "lousy debtor."

Consumer   "Fine, I'll write a check, but I'll have to post-date it for next month."

Collector   "That's fine lady, but if it doesn't clear the bank on that date, I'LL SUE YOU!"

Writing the post-dated check is OK, as long as she makes it good by the date on the check. A collector cannot state "I'll sue you" if he does not have the suit papers, the OK from the client to sue her, or have direct intentions to do so.

Showing signs of getting frustrated and angry, she gives the phone to her Supervisor.

Supervisor "Who is this?"

Collector "None of your business! Put Mary Jones back on the phone."

Supervisor "It *is* my business. My employees are not to receive any personal calls. You are *not* to call here again. Do you hear me?" (she hangs up on him)

Collector (calling back) "I want to speak to Mrs. Jones. Put her on, NOW!"

Supervisor (hangs up again)

Collector (calling back) ring, ring, ring, ring, ring, ring, ring, ring, ring, ring, ring, ring, ring, ring, ring, ring, ring . . . .

If the Collector is told by the Supervisor that he is not to call back, then he *cannot* call back. EVER! The Collector harassed the Supervisor and the Consumer by calling back when they hung up on him. Especially when he called back and let the phone ring and ring.

This phone call may be typical of one you've heard before, although there are parts of this conversation that are *illegal*. Unscrupulous Bill Collectors often speak and act this way, even though there are laws which prohibit their doing so. It is possible to expect lies, threats, shouting, and maybe even cussing at times. Most Collection Agencies are run professionally, but now and then there is "one" unscrupulous Collector who thinks he can get by with illegal tactics to make you pay your bill. Unfortunately, these tactics "usually" work because most Consumers don't know their RIGHTS.

The Consumer should not have had to endure the Collector's tactics. If the Collector had known that the Consumer understood the laws concerning the *Fair Debt Collection Practices Act,* he would have backed off immediately. He knows the consequences of using illegal tactics. Bill Collectors should always work on a professional level. Once you know the laws that protect you, you'll know how to handle the Collector who doesn't know how to handle himself.

While this conversation might have sounded a bit harsh, in reality, this is mild compared with what really is said, and the real language used. Lets face it though, most conversations between Collectors and Debtors are relatively mild.

Keep in mind that the Collector "walked all over" the Consumer, because she didn't know her RIGHTS. Had she known her RIGHTS, the Collector would have probably ended up in court, or she probably would have made an arrangement for $25 per month. The conversation was illegal.

This is only an example of what *could* and *does* happen when the conversation gets out of hand, especially when the Debtor does not know his RIGHTS.

1

The Account

The Placement Of Your Account With An Agency

The term CREDITOR means any person who offers or extends credit, creating a debt, or to whom a debt is owed. In other words—the CREDITOR is the company to whom you owe money.

The term DEBT means any obligation or alleged obligation of a consumer to pay money arising out of a transaction. DEBT is the amount of money you owe.

Federal law defines DEBT to mean: *"Any obligation or alleged obligation of a consumer to pay money arising out of a transaction in which the money, property, insurance, or services which are the subject of the transaction are primarily for personal, family or household purposes, whether or not such obligation has been reduced to judgment."*

The term CONSUMER means any natural person obligated or allegedly obligated to pay any debt for goods or services for personal use. This does not include business purchases. It includes the Consumer's spouse, parent (if the Consumer is a minor), guardian, executor, or administrator. CONSUMER means *you* if you owe money to a company.

A Creditor will only allow a bill to remain unpaid for so long. They will send numerous bills to you, with notification that you still have a balance due remaining on your bill. Finally, you will receive a warning letter stating that if the bill is not paid in a set amount of time, your account will be transferred to a Collection Agency. This is done as a last resort. The last thing the Creditor wants to do is to turn you in. They will have to pay a percentage of your bill to the Collection Agency (usually anywhere between 8% to 60%). That's a lot of money to pay someone to collect the money for them. It's better for the Creditor to get some of the money back through an agency, than to keep the account and get nothing at all. After 90-120 days without a payment, the Creditor will likely turn the account over to an agency. Usually, this is your last opportunity to pay the Creditor directly. You *are* obligated to pay the bill either from a service performed, goods purchased, or because of a legal and binding contract.

Interest Free Account

Normally, when an account is placed with an agency, the Creditor no longer allows interest to be added to the past due bill. However, this is not always true. The decision is up to the Creditor. If it is a government loan, count on interest still being added—especially Student Loans guaranteed by the government. Remember, any Creditor can charge interest while working with a Collection Agency. YOU SIGNED A CONTRACT! *Read it* to find out if interest may be legally added to your debt.

The following conduct is a violation of the law: The collection of any amount (including any interest, fee, charge, or expense incidental to the principal obligation) unless such amount is expressly authorized by the agreement creating the debt or permitted by law. In other words, a Collection Agency or Creditor cannot charge your account anything extra, unless your contract or the law specifically states that this can be done.

Furnishing Deceptive Forms

It is unlawful to design, compile, and furnish any form knowing that such form would be used to create the false belief in a Consumer that a person other than the Creditor of said Consumer is participating in the collection of or in an attempt to collect a debt said Consumer allegedly owes said Creditor, when in fact such person is not so participating. In other words: the Creditor is prohibited from purchasing dunning letters that falsely imply that a Debt Collector is collecting the debt, when in fact, only the Creditor is collecting.

Sample Letters:

TJC Collection Agency
P.O. Box 94
Smithville, CA 57799
007-555-7695

Date

Mr. John Doe
123 Cool Springs Dr.
Wedgeton, MI 99939

RE: The Jones Co.
777 Corner Stone Dr.
Smithville, CA 57799   ACCT #12345
007-555-7737   Balance Due: $500.00

The above Client has placed your account with our firm for payment in full. Either remit the balance immediately or contact our Client to make suitable arrangements.

If payment in full or arrangements are not made with our client, then we will continue with the collection process to protect our Client's interests.

Sincerely,
Mike Green

Unless you notify this office within 30 days after receiving this notice that you dispute the validity of the debt or any portion thereof, this office will assume this debt is valid. If you notify this office in writing within 30 days from receiving this notice, this office will: obtain verification of the debt or obtain a copy of a Judgement and mail you a copy of such Judgement or verification. If you request this office in writing within 30 days after receiving this notice, this office will provide you with the name and address of the original Creditor, if different from the current Creditor.

This is an attempt to collect a debt. Any information obtained will be used for that purpose.

This deceptive form implies there is a Collection Agency involved in this account, when in fact, the Creditor is the one who sent this letter. The give-away—their addresses are the same except for the Post Office box. The Creditor is having the mail directed to a P.O. Box. Also, notice how similar the phone numbers are. The Creditor could have a "special line" set up in the office for responses to these letters.

> TJC Collection Agency
> P.O. Box 94
> Smithville, California 57799
> 007-555-7695

Date

Mr. John Doe
123 Cool Springs Dr.
Wedgeton, Michigan 99939

RE: The Jones Co.
777 Corner Stone Dr.
Smithville, CA 57799   ACCT #12345
007-555-7737   Balance Due: $500.00

Please be advised that your account has been placed with our firm for collection.

The balance in full must be paid now. We are prepared to protect our client's interests. There is no need to contact us. Simply send your check or money order DIRECTLY TO OUR CLIENT, or telephone them to make suitable arrangements.

> Sincerely,
> *Mike Green*

Unless you notify this office within 30 days after receiving this notice that you dispute the validity of the debt or any portion thereof, this office will assume this debt is valid. If you notify this office in writing within 30 days from receiving this notice, this office will: obtain verification of the debt or obtain a copy of a Judgement and mail you a copy of such Judgement or verification. If you request this office in writing within 30 days after receiving this notice, this office will provide you with the name and address of the original Creditor, if different from the current Creditor.

This is an attempt to collect a debt. Any information obtained will be used for that purpose.

This deceptive form also implies there is a Collection Agency involved. Addresses again are similar, but in this case, they give you no way to talk directly with the Collection Agency (the Creditor's special line). They simply tell you to contact the Creditor directly.

These example letters to the Consumer are illegal and are not to be used by the Creditor, unless the letter expressly states that they are an "in-house Collection Agency." In other words, they must inform you that they *are* a part of the Jones Company, and are not a Collection Agency outside of the Jones Company paid to collect the debt.

2

The Search

Locating The Consumer Through Addresses And Phone Numbers

Post Office Boxes

Post Office boxes (used as home addresses) offer a real challenge to a Bill Collector. They have no way to locate neighbors with whom to leave a message to contact you. They will, however, call the Post Office to seek out a physical address. The Post Office *will not* give out this information, if it is used as a residential address. Some Collectors will attempt to leave a message with the Postal Carrier to take a message to the Consumer to have them call the agency (the Collector may only state their name and phone number). I have heard some Collectors go as far as calling the Post Office and claim to have a very large package to deliver to the Post Office box (which is too small to hold the package). They convince the Post Office to give out your physical address, so they can deliver the large package. Occasionally, the Post Office is conned into giving out your address. This trickery is against the law. If a Post Office box is used as a business address, then they'll freely give out your address. The Post Office has a privacy act that protects your physical address when you use a Post Office box as a residential address. You are paying for this Post Office box *and* the privacy. Make sure your Post Office knows that you expect your privacy enforced. If you're considering using a Post Office box as your address, then it will cost you approximately $30 per year.

Non-Published Numbers

Non-published numbers are frustrating to a Collector. The Bill Collector has no way to reach you at home by phone, only by letter. This pushes him into leaving messages with friends, neighbors, and relatives. You put the Bill Collector into a position in which he is forced to call you at work. He'll do his best to convince someone to give him your phone number. Your best bet is to give the Collector your number, so he'll not be forced to call everyone you know to convince them to give it to him. Is it worth going through the embarrassment? Face your bill instead of having to face everyone you know trying to explain what's going on. Under no circumstances can, or will the Telephone Operator give out your non-published number. You are paying for this service. This is your right. If a Collector tells you he obtained the non-published number from the Telephone Operator, he is lying. He obtained it by other means, probably from relatives, neighbors, friends, or even other Creditors to whom you have recently applied for credit.

Hours Of Calling

I have heard many people claim that a Bill Collector called them about their bill in the middle of the night. That's right, I'm talking 12 o'clock midnight, or even 3 o'clock in the morning.

Now, I'm not saying that's impossible, but I AM saying that it's highly improbable. Think about it, what person in his right mind would go all the way to work at 3 o'clock in the morning, just to call you up and harass you about your bill? Maybe, just maybe, you got an unscrupulous Collector that took your phone number home with him, and set his alarm for 3 o'clock in the morning so he could call you up and harass you. I don't think so. I would not believe he would be crazy enough to identify himself as the same person who calls you during the day. If he *does* identify himself as that same person, then I suggest you contact the Federal Trade Commission or the Attorney General in your state and make a complaint. They *will* investigate. These Government offices can check the Collection Agencies' long distance bills for that day and time, or even check the Collector's home phone bill for that same date and time. Maybe people exaggerate about the late hours in which they were called to sidestep the embarrassment of people knowing that a Bill Collector is calling them. Still, it's hard to believe this happens. Maybe they *are* being called in the middle of the night.

It is *illegal* for a Bill Collector to call you before 8:00 A.M., and after 9:00 P.M. YOUR TIME ZONE. No matter what time zone the Bill Collector is in, he can only call between 8:00 A.M. and 9:00 P.M. YOUR TIME ZONE. As usual, there is an exception to the rule. If you tell the Bill Collector or write him and give him permission to call you before or after these hours, then it is OK. This might be because you work nights, or leave very early in the morning and get home late from work. When you give him permission, be explicit on the hours during which he can call, otherwise he might take advantage and call whenever he wants. It *is* legal for the Collector to call you seven days a week, including major holidays and Sundays (if he were willing to work them).

Calling At An Inconvenient Time

Without the prior consent of the Consumer given directly to the Debt Collector or the express permission of a court of competent jurisdiction, a Debt Collector may not communicate with a Consumer in connection with the collection of any debt—at any unusual time or place, or at a time or place known or which should be known to be inconvenient to the Consumer. In the absence of knowledge of circumstances to the contrary, a Debt Collector shall assume that the convenient time for communicating with a Consumer is after 8 o'clock antimeridian and before 9 o'clock postmeridian, local time at the Consumer's location.

You have a right to privacy between 8:00 A.M. and 9:00 P.M. under certain conditions. Let's say you have your boss over for dinner, and a Bill Collector calls. All you have to do is say, "This is an inconvenient time," and ask that he call back at a later time. At that time he *must* cease conversation and obtain from you a better time in which to call. Other examples are: you are sick and in bed, a death in the family, the baby just fell and is hurt, and other miscellaneous emergencies.

Don't have too many excuses, because then it will be obvious that you are just trying to avoid his calls. This might aggravate him enough to attempt to get this bill paid through legal action. You'll have to speak to him some time, so face him and get it over with.

Time Zones

There are different time zones across the United States. The Bill Collector must recognize which time zone he is calling into, if calling into another state. For instance: If the Collection Agency is calling from Florida at 8:00 A.M. to California, then it is 5:00 in the morning in California. A Consumer must not be called at 5:00 A.M. just to talk about a bill. It's against the law, and against your legal rights. Sometimes the Collector isn't paying attention, and inadvertently calls into another time zone. Remember, mistakes can happen! He places hundreds of calls a day. He's bound to make a mistake once in a while. The first time he makes this type of call to you, it should be quietly dismissed. The Collector should apologize for the inconvenience, and call back at the appropriate time. You do not have to discuss the bill with him at this time unless you care to do so. If this earlier time is *not* an inconvenience, then you can tell the Collector it is all right to call you at this time. If it is not, then say so. If he contacts you earlier than 8:00 A.M. for the second time, against your wishes, you may push the issue. Call the owner of the Company and let him know that you're calling the FEDERAL TRADE COMMISSION or the ATTORNEY GENERAL. He knows you have proof of the illegal call by his long distance phone bill. Then do as you say you'll do, or wait for a response from the agency that states it will never happen again. This might even be a good time to bargain for a small payment arrangement, since you have him "over a barrel." He knows the law concerning times during which to call you. REMEMBER YOUR RIGHTS!

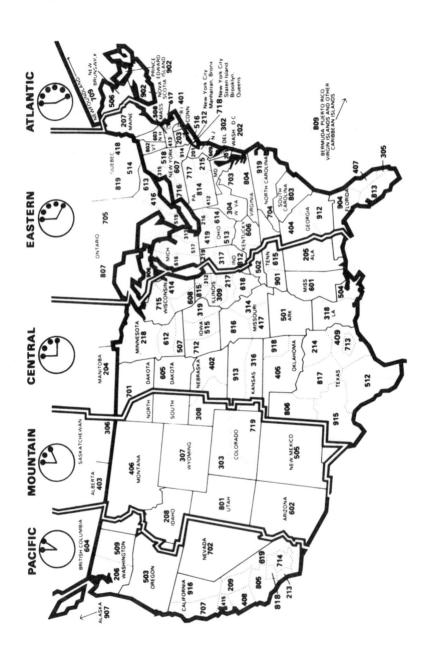

Answering Machines

Your answering machine can be a valuable tool. If you have an answering machine, put it to use. Some machines have a system set up to monitor the calls (check your instruction manual). As the person leaves a message on the recorder, you can hear his or her voice as they speak. If you want to talk to that person, just pick up the receiver and speak. If you don't recognize the voice on the recorder, then it's probably a Bill Collector or salesman anyway. If it *is* a Bill Collector, all he can do is leave his name, number, and company name. He *cannot* state anything about you owing a bill on this recording, or even that he is a Bill Collector or a Collection Agency. If you had a roommate or a friend check your messages for you on your recorder, then he is sure to hear that you owe a bill. That is THIRD PARTY DISCLOSURE. No one but the Collection Agency, the Creditor, and the one owing the money is to know about the bill. That's The Law! If a Collector gets a little too anxious to get in touch with you, he might get desperate and mention your bill, or say something offensive on your recorder. Don't get mad, you've got him on tape. Legal proof of third party disclosure, even abusive or threatening language. It's legal—he knew he was being recorded! If you feel the Collector is becoming "borderline illegal," then don't be afraid to ask him if it's OK to record the conversation. If he *does not* agree to the recording of the conversation, he probably has something to hide. If you have a taped conversation of a Bill Collector that you feel is evidence of illegal actions by a Bill Collector, take it to the Attorney General's office. They will see to it that the situation is taken care of.

Phone Number Con Game

Conning phone numbers out of children, friends, and relatives is a common occurrence, and is a tactic used by many Bill Collectors. The problem is, these people are unsuspecting and are eager to help this person get in touch with the Debtor. They are left with the impression that the Collector is really a friend, co-worker, relative, or they have important information for that person. Sometimes the word "emergency" arises, and these people are only too anxious to help. They don't have any idea that this is a Bill Collector in search of a Debtor. Beware of friendly Collectors, or Collectors that claim to have important information for the Debtor. They will be very sneaky at obtaining information on your home and work numbers. Warn these people if you can, not to disclose any information to anyone they don't know or recognize. Most importantly, (as you will read in chapter 3), the Collector is *not* allowed to disclose to any of these people, the fact that he is calling in reference to a debt that you owe.

3

The Contact

Communication between
the Consumer and the Collector

First Letter Notification

Within five days after the initial communication with a Consumer in connection with the collection of any debt, a Debt Collector shall, unless the following information is contained in the initial communication or the Consumer has paid the debt, send the Consumer a written notice containing:

(1) The amount of the debt.

(2) The name of the Creditor to whom the debt is owed.

(3) A statement that unless the Consumer, within thirty days after receipt of the notice, disputes the validity of the debt, or any portion thereof, the debt will be assumed to be valid by the Debt Collector.

(4) A statement that if the Consumer notifies the Debt Collector in writing within the thirty-day period that the debt, or any portion thereof, is disputed, the Debt Collector will obtain verification of the debt or a copy of a Judgement will be mailed to the Consumer by the Debt Collector.

(5) A statement that, upon the Consumer's written request within the thirty-day period, the Debt Collector will provide the Consumer with the name and address of the original Creditor, if different from the current Creditor.

Once a Collection Agency contacts you about your bill by telephone, they are required by law to send a letter to you notifying you of the placement of your account with their agency. This must be done within 5 days, unless you have paid the debt, or statements 1 thru 5 above have been communicated to you orally. You will not always receive this letter on schedule or at all. For instance, if you have recently moved, the letter will have to be forwarded to your new address. This takes time. Maybe the letter they sent you was returned by the Post Office because you left no forwarding address, or the forwarding order at the Post Office had expired. As long as they sent it, their legal obligation is met. Once you *are* located, then the letter *must* be resent *immediately*. This "first letter" sent to you by the Creditor will have a notice about disputing the debt, as you will see in the bottom half of the next 2 letters.

In the following three sample letters, the first one is legal. and contains the appropriate wording and information on the letter per the FAIR DEBT COLLECTION PRACTICES ACT. The last two letters are plainly and simply-*illegal*. If you ever receive a letter similar to the latter two, take them immediately to your Attorney. Also, send a copy directly to the Attorney General and Federal Trade Commission in your state.

XYZ Collections
#1 Park Street
Red Park, California 93777
007-555-7695

Date

John Doe   RE: The Jones Company
123 Cool Springs Drive   ACCT #12345
Wedgetone, Michigan 99939   Balance due: $500

Be Advised! This account has been placed in our office for Collection. Accounts placed for collection are automatically reported to the Credit Bureau. The FAIR CREDIT REPORTING ACT states that such adverse information can remain in your credit file for a seven year period.

If payment in full is received now, it will prevent your account from being reported to the Credit Bureau.

Unless you notify this office within 30 days after receiving this notice that you dispute the validity of the debt or any portion thereof, this office will assume this debt is valid. If you notify this office in writing within 30 days from receiving this notice, this office will: obtain verification of the debt or obtain a copy of a Judgement and mail you a copy of such Judgement or verification. If you request this office in writing within 30 days after receiving this notice, this office will provide you with the name and address of the original Creditor, if different from the current Creditor.

Sincerely,
Mike Green

Many Collection Agencies do not report your credit information to the Credit Bureau. In the case of this letter, they *are* a Credit Reporting Collection Agency. If they were not a reporting Collection Agency, then this letter would be illegal.

XYZ Collections
#1 Park Street
Red Park, California 93777
007-555-7695

Date

John Doe   RE: The Jones Company
123 Cool Springs Drive   ACCT #12345
Wedgeton, Michigan 99939   Balance due: $500

Your account has been placed with our firm for recovery of the full balance. You have not responded to our attempts to call you. You have shown a lack of desire to fulfill your obligation to our client, therefore you have 48 hours in which to make suitable arrangements with us, or pay the consequences. Deadbeats like yourself usually need more persuasion. Cease with your irresponsible ways, and contact us immediately.

Sincerely,
Mike Green

Did you feel threatened or insulted after reading this letter? I was embarrassed when I wrote it. Unfortunately, lawsuits have been filed against Collection Agencies for this type of letter. They don't exist as much as they used to, but they *do* exist. This collection letter is out and out harassing and abusive. The Collector threatened you with "48 HOURS" and "PAYING THE CONSEQUENCES." What are these consequences? What if you don't pay in 48 hours? A Bill Collector may not call you names like "DEADBEAT," and accuse you of being irresponsible. This letter is abusive, oppressive, harassing, and is suable in Court.

XYZ Collections
#1 Park Street
Red Park, California 93777
007-555-7695

Date

John Doe   RE: The Jones Company
123 Cool Springs Drive   ACCT #12345
Wedgeton, Michigan 99939   Balance due: $500

Your account has been placed with our firm for collections. Please remit the balance in full immediately or contact us to make suitable arrangements.

Failure to do so, will result in contacting your employer. This could be highly embarrassing. A garnishment of your wages could cause you to be dismissed from your job. Spare yourself this embarrassment and pay the balance immediately.

Sincerely,
Mike Green

This letter is threatening to contact a third party (your employer) to disclose to them that you owe on a bill. It also implies your wages will be garnished and you'll lose your job because of it.

(1) They cannot contact your employer about your bill.

(2) They cannot threaten to garnish your wages.

(3) You cannot lose your job for ONE garnishment of your wages.

In both of the last two letters, the *Fair Debt Collection Practices Act* notice at the bottom of the letter is missing. The first of these three letters has this notice at the bottom of the letter. It is required by law to have this notice placed on the *first* letter that your receive.

Disputed Debts

If the Consumer notifies the Debt Collector in writing within a thirty day period (from the date of the first notification sent by the agency) that the debt, or any portion thereof, is disputed, or that the Consumer requests the name and address of the original Creditor, the Debt Collector shall *cease collection of the debt, or any disputed portion thereof*, until the Debt Collector obtains verification of the original Creditor, and a copy of such verification or judgment, or name and address of the original Creditor, is mailed to the Consumer by the Debt Collector.

The failure of a Consumer to dispute the validity of a debt, may not be construed by any court as an admission or liability by the Consumer.

Once a Debt Collector knows the Consumer is represented by an Attorney about this debt, and has knowledge of or can readily ascertain such Attorney's name and address, he cannot communicate with any person other than the Attorney, unless the Attorney fails to respond to the Bill Collector within a reasonable period of time. A Debt Collector who knows a Consumer is represented by an Attorney with respect to a DEBT, is not required to assume similar representation on other debts. However, if a Consumer notifies the Debt Collector that the Attorney has been retained to represent him for *all* current and future debts that may be placed with the Debt Collector, the Debt Collector must deal only with that Attorney.

If you are being billed for a product or service that was faulty or incomplete, again, you have rights. Write a certified letter to both the Creditor and the Collection Agency, lodging this complaint. If it's a legitimate dispute, the Creditor should clear up the problem or pull the account from the Agency. This doesn't always happen. The majority of the time the Creditor claims no responsibility, and feels the placement of the bill to the Agency is a due response. If there is a definite dispute, contact the Better Business Bureau or an Attorney. A hold will be placed on collection activity until the dispute is resolved. A Bill Collector cannot contact the Consumer in any form about the bill as long as the dispute is in effect, or an Attorney has been retained. The Collector will contact the Attorney, and the Attorney must respond to the Collector about the debt within a reasonable amount of time. If this time is exceeded, then collection activity may resume. The Collector and Attorney will try to work out the dispute and usually come to a mutual agreement—sometimes a settlement, a smaller payment arrangement, or even have the Creditor drop the bill all together. The following two letters are examples of dispute letters sent to the Collection Agency.

123 Cool Springs Drive
Wedgeton, Michigan 99939

Date

XYZ Collections   RE: Auto Repair Center
#1 Park Street   ACCT #12345
Red Park, California 93777   Balance due: $400.00

Dear Mr. Green:

Per the FAIR DEBT COLLECTION PRACTICES ACT, I have the right to send this letter to DISPUTE the validity of this debt. I am requesting that you contact Mr. Smith my Attorney regarding this bill. He is representing me in this dispute. Please contact him at 500 Carmel Street, Bluebox, California 67474, 1-800-999-9999.

Sincerely,
John Doe

This letter is the simple approach when you have Attorney representation. The Collection Agency may only contact the Attorney if they have any questions.

123 Cool Springs Drive
Wedgeton, Michigan 99939

Date

XYZ Collections   RE: Auto Repair Center
#1 Park Street   ACCT #12345
Red Park, California 93777   Balance due: $400.00

Dear Mr. Green:

Per the FAIR DEBT COLLECTION PRACTICES ACT I have the right to send this letter to DISPUTE the validity of this debt. My car was brought in for repair of the brake system. The Auto Repair Center fixed my brakes as requested, and without my permission, put 4 new tires on my car. I am asking for proof that I requested these 4 tires in addition to the brake work. I will pay for the tires when proof is shown that I ordered them. My total bill is $700. Enclosed is a check in the amount of $300 for the brake work. The remaining $400 is in dispute and I am requesting that you contact your client and validate this debt.

Sincerely,
John Doe

The Collector will accept the check for $300 to pay off the undisputed portion of the bill, but may not continue collection on the disputed portion of the bill. He must then contact the Creditor to try to resolve the dispute. The Creditor will either provide proof of the order for the tires, or remove the account from collection.

When a Bill Collector First Calls

When a Bill Collector calls you, he *must* first do three things:

(1) Identify himself (A Debt Collector may use an ALIAS if it is used consistently and it does not interfere with another party's ability to identify him. e.g., the true identity can be ascertained).

(2) Identify his company.

(3) Identify the bill he is representing.

(An ALIAS is an assumed name used by Bill Collectors to protect the true identity of the Collector). When I first started collecting bills, I used my real name an saw nothing wrong with it. I was soon convinced to use an ALIAS to protect myself. Why protect myself? Too many stories circulated about a Debtor wanting to get EVEN with a Collector, by calling him at home and even going to the Collector's home and threaten his life. It's sad but true. The Collector never knows when he'll contact an irate person. The Collector is allowed by law to use an ALIAS.

I have heard people state that a Collector called them about their bill and refused to identify their name or their company name. This *does* happen, and for a reason. A Collector can scare you into paying the bill directly to the Creditor. It doesn't matter to the Collector whether you pay the Agency or the Creditor. He still gets his commission. BY LAW, he *must* identify his name, company name, and the bill he is representing.

If you are *not* the person he is searching for, and you ask his name, he *must* identify himself by name. If asked, he *must* give the initials of the company, like "I'm calling for XYZ." Just ask him what the initials stand for. Then ask him "Is this a Collection Agency?" He will either avoid the question or say, "It's personal business." He *must* answer the question. The Collector Must *Always* Tell The Truth.

Third Party Disclosure

Any Debt Collector communication with any person other than the Consumer for the purpose of acquiring location information about the Consumer shall:

(1) Identify himself, state that he is confirming or correcting location information concerning the Consumer, and, only if expressly requested, identify his employer.

(2) Not state that such Consumer owes any debt.

(3) Not communicate with any such person more than once unless requested to do so by such person or unless the Debt Collector reasonably believes that the earlier response of such person is erroneous or incomplete and that such person now has correct or complete location information.

Although the *Fair Debt Collection Practices Act* generally protects the Consumer's privacy by limiting Debt Collector communications about personal affairs to third parties, it recognizes the need for some third party contact by Collectors to seek the where-abouts of the Consumer. The intent of Congress is to protect the Consumer's privacy rights by prohibiting Debt Collectors from communicating a Consumer's personal affairs to a third party.

Third party disclosure means telling someone other than the one who owes the money about your bill, or telling someone other than the owner of the credit card about the bill owed. THS IS ILLEGAL. It is illegal plainly and simply to tell anyone about someone else's bill. However, there is one exception to the rule. *You must give permission to the Bill Collector* either in person, by phone, or by letter that it is OK for them to talk to a specific person about your bill. Example: "You can talk to my father about my bill, he'll be helping me out financially." Telephone answering machines can be used as third party disclosure. Example: leaving a message on a recorder that states "This is Mike with XYZ Collections, and I'm calling about your deliquent account with BUD'S REPAIR SERVICE. Call me at 1-800-123-4567." The reason this is possible third party disclosure is: what if someone other than the one owing the bill happened to overhear this recording? Perhaps your roommate came home from work and checked his messages on the machine, and overheard your delinquency. This information is for YOU and YOU ONLY. It is no one else's business but yours. Another example is when calling upon a neighbor to give a message to you. They cannot disclose to this third party that this is about your past due bill. The Bill Collector should just give his name, phone number, and company (if asked), and ask that you call him back. *This is all that should be given.*

Once a Debt Collector learns a Consumer is represented by an Attorney, he must limit his request for location information to the Attorney.

A Debt Collector is not to communicate with you by post card (the Postman or the person handling the mail could read on the card that you are delinquent on a bill). They are not to use any language or symbol on any envelope or in the contents of any communication effected by the mails or telegram that indicates that the Debt Collector is in the Debt Collection business or that the communication is related to the collection of a debt. In other words, when you look at the envelope, you should not be able to tell in any way that this is from a Collection Agency.

What about using other symbols on the envelope that don't pertain to collections? In today's world, advertisers are trying anything and everything to get Consumers to open and read the billions and billions of advertisements sent to households across the country. If people don't open the envelopes, then they'll never know about the sales going on or a new product on the market. They spend billions of dollars a year on advertising through the mail. Getting the letter there is no problem, the problem is getting you to open and read the letter. So, how do they make you open it? By printing on the outside of the envelope "YOU WIN," or "NATIONAL PRIZE DISTRIBUTION CENTER." How about the ones I always disappointedly open— the ones that appear to have a CHECK enclosed "PAY TO THE ORDER OF DAVID L. KELCHER Jr." It's all a CON to get you to open the envelope.

Collectors do the same thing. It's purely and simply illegal, but it still happens today. The idea, again, is to get you to open the letter and pay your bill. If the envelope appears to be from the Government would you open it? Most people would. Some agencies will use symbols such as the *scales of justice,* a symbol appearing to be a police badge, a silhouette of a Judge, or even a Judge's gavel. I don't know about you, but I would certainly open an envelope with those type symbols on it. These symbols are a false misrepresentation of the agency, and are even implying that you are being sued, or that this is an Official Notice. If you ever get a letter like this, I suggest you take it directly to your Attorney, the Federal Trade Commission, or the Attorney General for your state. After this is done, just sit back and watch what happens. I doubt you'll ever hear from that Agency again.

Calling You At Work

Many people believe that it is against the law for a Collection Agency to call you on your job. This is wrong. A collector *can* call you at your place of employment. This is perfectly legal. However, there are stipulations. If the Bill Collector is told you cannot receive personal calls at work, then he *cannot* call you at work. This is usually told to him by the person answering the phone, the Supervisor, or the personnel office. If he is told you cannot receive calls, then he will attempt to leave a message. A Debt Collector may not call the Consumer at work if he has a reason to believe the employer forbids such communication.

Some Collectors are very persistent. They will try to convince the person who answered the phone that it is very urgent or important, and that they put him through to you right away. Rarely, an unscrupulous Collector will try to sneak in the word "EMERGENCY" to get the call through to you. That word (said by a Bill Collector) is against the law, and cannot be used. If the word EMEREGENCY is used, then get the name of the person he said it to, and contact the Federal Trade Commission or the Attorney General in your state. Since the word EMERGENCY cannot be used, then most Collectors tend to use the word "URGENT" or "VERY IMPORTANT."

Bill Collectors calling you at work may cause you to lose your job. It always seems that "when it rains, it pours." If one Collector is calling you at work, then chances are others are calling too. Too many personal calls for one person can irritate personnel, the operator, or the Supervisor. Don't be surprised if you are summoned into the office to discuss these calls. It could be a highly embarrassing discussion. One suggestion is to have your Supervisor tell the caller to stop calling. He *must* adhere to her words, and cannot call back again. The Collector must not pressure anyone at your job to put you on the phone. This could be construed as third party harassment (harassing someone other than the person owing the money).

If your place of employment is the only place the Collector can reach you, and he is told he cannot call you at work, then he might get frustrated enough to try to SUE you. At this point, he could call the Creditor he is doing the work for and convince him that you are avoiding both the Creditor and paying the bill, and that it is necessary to send you the signed suit papers. His next step would be to call the personnel department to verify your position, length of employment, income, and the address to your work. This information could possibly be used to file for legal action. If he's convinced you're trying to avoid him and your bill, then you can't blame him for trying to get a judgment against you. When possible try to talk to him if he calls you at work, or return his calls if he leaves a message. If you can't call him while at work, then call him when you get home. If you don't face him, then you're asking for trouble.

Hang-Ups

Picture this: A Bill Collector calls you about your bills and half way through the conversation he makes you mad and you hang up on him. He calls you back and you hang up on him again. The third time he calls, you just let the phone ring and ring and ring. What would YOU do in this situation? Most people would just hang up on him again, or just let the phone ring. Remember this: **if you hang up on a Bill Collector, he can not call you back.** Remember though, he can still call you back at a later date. If it were an accidental disconnection, then he has the right to call you back. If a Collector calls back after you hang up on him, then it *is* harassment. Record the date and time this happened and relay the information to your Attorney.

Ceasing Communication

If a Consumer notifies a Debt Collector *in writing* that the Consumer refuses to pay a debt or that the Consumer wishes the Debt Collector to cease further communication with the Consumer, the Debt Collector shall not communicate further with the Consumer with respect to such debt, except:

(1) To advise the Consumer that the Debt Collector's further efforts are being terminated.

(2) To notify the Consumer that the Debt Collector or Creditor may invoke specified remedies which are ordinarily invoked by such Debt Collector or Creditor.

(3) Where applicable, to notify the Consumer that the Debt Collector or Creditor intends to invoke a specified remedy. If such notice from the Consumer is made by mail, notification shall be complete upon receipt.

You have a right whether or not you are to be contacted by phone or mail about your bill. You can be called and will receive letters notifying you about your bill, but you can stop this contact if you want to, by writing a letter to the Agency stating:

123 Cool Springs Drive
Wedgeton, MIchigan 99939

Date

XYZ Collections	RE: The Jones Company
#1 Park Street	ACCT #12345
Red Park, California 93777	Balance due: $500

Dear Mr. Green:
   This letter is in reference to my bill owed to The Jones
Company, Account number 12345. I am exercising my
rights per the FAIR DEBT COLLECTION PRACTICES
ACT (section 805) by asking that you cease communication
with me about this bill, both by letter and by phone. This
includes my residence and my place of employment. A copy
of this letter is retained by myself along with the CERTIFIED
MAIL receipt. By law, this is the only notification you need.

Sincerely yours
John Doe

   They may, however, call or write you one final time after
receiving your letter. They will call to advise you that they
are in receipt of your letter and will cease communication
with you. They may also state that since you wish them
to cease communication with you, they are going to attempt
to obtain the money legally (if law allows in your state,
and with the client's permission). Communication must also
cease if you simply write a letter stating you *refuse* to pay
the debt. THIS IS YOUR RIGHT! Use it if you want, but
if they can't talk or write to you about the bill, then they
just might have to call the Creditor and get permission
to take legal action against you. They will be forced to
state that you are avoiding this bill and the only recourse
is a CIVIL SUIT. So be careful, don't put them in that
situation unless you have a very good reason.

Key Words

Don't be afraid of what the Collector says. The main objective of the unscrupulous Collector is to intimidate you, confuse you, and scare you into paying your bill. After you pay your debt, he'll move on to another unsuspecting Debtor.

Most people hear the words LITIGATION and jump to conclusions. They don't actually hear what is being said. They just tune in to the words that scare them the most. Read the next sentence carefully; "I'm processing your PAPERWORK towards LITIGATION. Do you have an Attorney?" Now, after reading the preceding statement and question, are you being sued? Of course not! He is *processing* your PAPERWORK *towards* LITIGATION. The fact that he asked if you had an Attorney was irrelevant. It was just an attempt to make the first statement imply that you ARE being sued. It is absolutely against the law to leave the Consumer with the impression that he is being sued. Isn't that exactly what he has done? If he were really suing you, you would know it. But in this case, he really stated that he was just going through the normal collection procedures. Again, read the following sentence carefully. "Obviously you're not going to settle your account on a voluntary basis, so I'm going to recommend to my client that we sue you immediately." What's the key word? RECOMMEND. Just pay attention to what he is saying, and don't be afraid to ask him to CLARIFY what he IS saying. For instance, "Am I really being sued or are you just trying to scare me? If he says he IS going to sue you then he had better have the suit papers in hand, or have the definite intentions to do so, as you'll see in the next section.

They Can't Say What They Won't Do

A Collector cannot say he IS going to do something if he does not intend to do it. If he says he IS suing you, then he better do it, intend to do it, or have permission from the Creditor. However he CAN say he will RECOMMEND that civil action be taken. This is a legal way to scare you. Recommendations to a Creditor for suit aren't always agreed to. This depends on whether you are not paying anything at all, the size of your bill, and who the Creditor is.

It is illegal to take or threaten to take any nonjudicial action to effect dispossession or disablement of property if:

(1) There is no present right to possession of the property claimed as collateral through an enforceable security interest.

(2) There is no *present intention* to take possession of the property.

(3) The property is exempt by law from such dispossession or disablement.

The following information should explain what was said in the previous paragraph: A Debt Collector may not state that he will take any action unless he intends to take the action when the statement was made, or ordinarily takes the action in similar cirmcumstances. A Debt Collector may not state or imply that he or any third party may take any action unless such action is legal and there is a reasonable likelihood, at the time the statement was made, that such action will be taken. A Debt Collector *may* state that certain action is possible, if it is true that such action is legal and is frequently taken by the Collector or Creditor with respect to similar debts; however, if the Creditor has reason to know there are facts that make the action unlikely in the particular case, to state the action was possible would be misleading. A Debt Collector may not threaten to report a dishonored check or other fact to the police, unless he actually intends to take this action. A Debt Collector may not threaten to attach a Consumer's tax refund when he has no authority to do so.

THREAT OF LEGAL OR OTHER ACTION. This section (807 in the summary), refers not only to a false threat of legal action, but also a false threat by a Debt Collector that he will report a debt to a Credit Bureau, assess a collection fee, or undertake any other action if the debt is not paid. A Debt Collector may also not misrepresent the imminence of such action. A Debt Collector's implication, as well as direct statement, of planned legal action may be an unlawful deception. For example, reference to an Attorney or to legal proceedings may mislead the Debtor as to the likelihood or imminence of legal action. A Debt Collector's statement that legal action has been recommended is a representation that legal action may be taken, since such a recommendation implies that the Creditor will act on it at least some of the time. Lack of intent may be inferred when the amount of the debt is so small as to make the action totally unfeasible, or when the Debt Collector is unable to take the action because the Creditor has not authorized him to do so.

ILLEGALITY OF THREATENED ACT. A Debt Collector may not threaten that he will contact an employer, or other third party, or take some other "action that cannot be legally taken" (such as advising the Creditor to sue where such advise would violate state rules governing the unauthorized practice of law). If state law forbids a Debt

Collector from suing in his own name (or from doing so without first obtaining formal assignment of the account, and that has not been done), the Debt Collector may not represent that he will sue in that state. A Debt Collector may not falsely state that the Consumer's account will be referred back to the original Creditor, who would not be bound by the Fair Debt Collection Practices Act. This threat could imply that the original Creditor could "legally harass the Consumer" and do basically anything he wants to the Consumer.

Don't allow a Collector to walk all over you with empty threats. If he makes a threat that you feel is illegal, then make a few calls to verify that these are legitimate. Call the Creditor to see if they have given authorization to the Collector to follow through with the threat. Call Trans-Union or TRW (credit bureau agencies) to see if the Collection Agency is a reporting agency. Just becuase they are a Collection Agency does not mean that they can report your delinquency to the Credit Bureau. Don't be afraid to do a little checking up on them. They check on you!

False Or Misleading Representations

A Debt Collector may not use any false, deceptive, or misleading representation or means in connection with the collection of any debt. Without limiting the general application of the foregoing, the following conduct is a violation of this section:

(1) The false representation or implication that the Debt Collector is vouched for, bonded by or affiliated with the United States and/or State, including the use of any badge, uniform, or facsimile thereof. A Debt Collector may not use a symbol in correspondence that makes him appear to be a Government official. For example, a Collection letter depicting a Police badge, a Judge, or the *scales of justice.*

(2) The false representation of—
   (A) The character, amount, or legal status of any debt (A Debt Collector may not send a collection letter from a "Pre-legal Department," where no Legal Department exists. An Attorney may use a computer service to send letters on his own behalf, but a Debt Collector may not send a computer generated letter using an Attorney's name).

   (B) Any services rendered or compensation which may be lawfully received by any Debt Collector for the collection of a debt.

(3) The false representation or implication that any individiual is an Attorney or that any communication is from an Attorney. A Debt Collector may not falsely represent that a person named in a letter is an Attorney.

(4) The representation or implication that non-payment or any debt will result in the arrest or imprisonment of any person or the seizure, garnishment, attachment, or sale of any property or wages of any person unless such action is lawful and the Debt Collector or Creditor intends to take such action.

(5) The threat to take any action that cannot legally be taken or that is not intended to be taken.

(6) The false representation or implication that a sale, referral, or other transfer of any interest in a debt shall cause the Consumer to—

(A) Lose any claim or defense to payment of the debt

(B) Become subject to any practices prohibited by the following:

(7) The false representation or implication that the Consumer committed any crime or other conduct in order to disgrace the Consumer. A Debt Collector may not falsely allege that the Consumer has committed fraud. A Debt Collector may not make a misleading statement of law, falsely implying that the Consumer has committed a crime, or mischaracterize what constitutes an offense by misstating or omitting significant elements of the offense. For example, a Debt Collector may not tell the Consumer that he has committed a crime by issuing a check that is dishonored, when the stature applies only where there is a "scheme to defraud."

(8) Communicating or threatening to communicate to any person credit information which is known or which should be known as to be false, including the failure to communicate that a disputed debt is disputed.

(9) The use or distribution of any written communication which simulates or is falsely represented to be a

document authorized, issued, or approved by any court, official, or agency of the United States or any State, or which creates a false impression as to its source, authorization or approval. For instance; sending a letter that gives the impression that this letter is a legal document authorized by the Police Department, a Government Official, the State, or even the Courts.

(10) The use of any false representation or deceptive means to collect or attempt to collect any debt or to obtain information concerning a Consumer. A Debt Collector may not communicate by a format or envelope that misrepresents the nature, purpose, or urgency of the message. It is a violation to send any communication that conveys to the Consumer a false sense of urgency. A Debt Collector may not mislead the Consumer as to the legal consequences of the Consumer's actions (e.g., by implying that a failure to respond is an admission of liability). He also may not falsely state or imply that a Consumer is required to assign his wages to his Creditor when he is not, that the Debt Collector has counseled the Creditor to sue when he has not, that adverse credit information has been entered on the Conusumer's credit record when it has not, that the entire amount is due when there is no acceleration clause, or that he cannot accept partial payments when in fact he is authorized to accept them.

(11) Except as otherwise provided for communications to acquire location information under section 1692b of the Fair Debt Collection Practices Act, the failure to disclose clearly in all communications made to collect a debt or to obtain information about a Consumer, that the Debt Collector is attempting to collect a debt and that any information obtained will be used for that purpose.

(12) The false representation or implication that accounts have been turned over to innocent purchasers for value.

(13) The false representation or implication that documents are legal process.

(14) The use of any business, company, or organization name other than the true name of the Debt Collector's business, company, or organization. A DEBT COLLECTION BUSINESS must use its real business name, commonly used name, or acronym in both written and oral communications. A CREDITOR may not use any name that would falsely imply that a third party is involved in the collection. The *in-house* collections unit of "ABC Corp." may use the name of "ABC Collection Division," but not the name "XYZ Collection Agency" or some other unrelated name.

(15) The false representation or implication that documents are not legal process forms or do not require action by the Consumer.

(16) The false representation or implicaiton that a Debt Collector operates or is employed by a Consumer Reporting Agency.

Watch out for a fancy talking Collector. He might use legal terms freely and sound like an Attorney, but he is not! For example; "Our firm has been retained. . . . . " A Collection Agency IS a firm and they have been retained, but this is to confuse you into thinking they are an Attorney's office. This is an illegal tactic. He cannot tell you that he IS an Attorney, if he is not. That is also illegal. Don't be afraid to say; "You are not an Attorney." THERE ARE COLLECTION ATTORNEYS. Be sure he is a legitimate Attorney.

Harassment

A Debt Collector may not engage in any conduct the natural consequence of which is to harass, oppress, or abuse any person in connection with the collection of a debt. Without limiting the general application of the foregoing, the following conduct is a violation of this section:

(1) The use or threat of use of violence or other criminal means to harm the physical person, reputation, or property of any person.

(2) The use of obscene or profane language or language of which the natural consequence is to abuse the hearer or reader.

(3) The publication of a list of Consumers who allegedly refuse pay debts, except to a Consumer Reporting Agency or to persons meeting the requirements.

(4) The advertisement for sale of any debt to coerce payment of the debt.

(5) Causing a telephone to ring or engaging any person in telephone conversation repeatedly or continuously with intent to annoy, abuse or harass any person at the called number.

(6) The placement of telephone calls without meaningful disclosure of the caller's identity.

HARASSMENT:

To disturb or irritate PERSISTENTLY, to wear out, exhaust, to enervate (an enemy) by repeated raids (from the American Heritage Dict. 1979). A lot of people claim that they are being HARASSED by the Collector, because he is calling them about their bill. Wrong! Just because he is calling you, you can't claim harassment. Does he call you *every day*, make your phone ring and ring when you hang up on him? Does he hang up when you answer the phone? The following are more harassment techniques: A Debt Collector leaving telephone messages with many different neighbors when he knows the Consumer's name and telephone number and could have reached him directly. A Debt Collector engaging in repeated personal contacts with a Consumer with such frequency as to harass him. For example: he will follow the Consumer or contact him six times in one day. He cannot pose a lengthy series of questions or comments to the Consumer without giving the Consumer a chance to reply. He cannot imply a threat of violence. For example, the Collector will pressure a Consumer with statements such as "We're not playing around here—we can play TOUGH,"or "We're going to send somebody to collect for us one way or another." A Collector will threaten to SHAME a Consumer into payment by publicizing the debt. A Bill Collector may not: exchange lists of Consumers who allegedly refuse to pay their debts, may not distribute a list of alleged Debtors to his credit subscribers, because the statute permits him to provide such information only to Consumer Reporting Agencies, and may not use a false business name in a phone call to conceal his identity.

Before you present a formal complaint to an Attorney, be sure it *IS* harassment. Beware, harassment is hard to prove. Long distance phone calls are easy to prove. The long distance call is recorded on the Collection Agency's phone bill, and with the Phone Company.

If necessary, your Attorney can obtain this information for your case.

Vulgar Language Or Name Calling

Name calling is unacceptable in the practice of Bill Collecting. A Bill Collector cannot call you and use curse words, Period! You don't have to listen to that. Just hang up the phone. Other ways he can intimidate you is to down-grade you. For instance, calling you a FREELOADER, DEADBEAT, LOWLY, or anything of the such is illegal— especially if it down-grades your ethnic background. Abusive language includes religious slurs, profanity, obscenity, calling the Consumer a liar or a deadbeat, and the use of racial or sexual epithets. Their job is not to cut you down, but to collect the bill. If you have problems with this, then report this action immediately to your Attorney or the Federal Trade Commission. Again, you should have proof. Remember, it's your word against theirs. It's very hard to prove such language was used. A Bill Collector *may* call you a Debtor, because you *do* owe money, but watch his tone of voice, he could be cutting you down.

I have seen many times when after a Debtor hangs up on a Collector, the Debtor calls back and asks for the Supervisor. He states that a Collector called and abused him with his vulgar language. The Debtor will repeat curse words that the Collector used against the Debtor. Rarely have I ever seen a Collector use abusive and vulgar language. The Supervisor is within listening distance of all Collectors and monitors most of their calls to be sure they stay within the guidelines of the law. When a Debtor complains of the vulgar language used to the Supervisor, it ruins the Debtor's credibility, because 99 times out of 100, the Debtor is lying or exaggerating, and trying to get the Collector into trouble. Unless you have a valid complaint, don't bother the Supervisor. He's heard exaggerations before. If you can capture the moment on tape, then I'm sure you'll be able to get the Supervisor's attention.

4

The Payment

Negotiating Payments and Saving Money

Multiple Debts

If any Consumer owes multiple debts and makes any single payment to any Debt Collector with respect to such debts, said Debt Collector may not apply such payment to any debt which is disputed by the Consumer, and where applicable, shall apply such payment in accordance with the Consumer's directions. Example: if a Consumer has more than one account placed with the same Collection Agency and he sends in $50, the Consumer has the right to state which account the money is to be credited against. For instance, he can state, "$25 to each account" or "$50 to account 'A' and nothing to account 'B.'" If you fail to note how much money is applied to each account, then it is usually divided up equally between both accounts. You have the right to say how much money is applied to which account. If one of the accounts is in dispute, then any money sent in *must be* applied to the good account. The disputed account *must not* have any money applied to it until the account has been proven by the original Creditor to be legitimate and is taken out of the disputed status.

The Big Lie

A common misconception that seems to have swept the nation is the big lie that states, "As long as I pay *something* or at least show an *effort* in paying my bill, then there is nothing anyone can do to me." Wrong! This rumor was started by someone who did not know what he was talking about. Don't ever tell a Bill Collector that there is nothing he can do. He's liable to show you what he CAN do. The Collection Agency can sue you if the Creditor OK's it. What do you think a signed contract is for? It protects the Creditors' RIGHTS to their money.

Payment Arrangements

A Bill Collector is trained to put as much pressure as possible on you to pay your entire balance all at once. Rarely will you find a Collector who will allow a payment arrangement the first time he contacts you. Usually, by the third or forth time speaking with you, he realizes that it is virtually hopeless to get you to pay the entire $500 all in one check. This is the time he will back down from his strong demands and try to work out a suitable arrangement. The arrangements are usually suitable only to him (probably $250 per month). It is your job to convince him that your finances aren't capable of supporting $250 per month, or even the regular monthly payments of your original contract. If your situation is such that there is not enough money available to make full payments to your Creditor, then what makes them think that you can make them to the Bill Collector!

The key to a successful payment arrangement is to be nice to the Bill Collector. No matter what he says, or how he acts, BITE YOUR TONGUE! It's always to your advantage to be on his good side. Never lie or exaggerate to the Collector. He's heard ALL of the excuses, lies, exaggerations, and cliche's possible. He doesn't want to hear that you, "Can't get blood out of a turnip." "I've been unemployed for the past 6 months." "I'm at the end of receiving my unemployment benefits." "They are getting ready to shut off my electric and phone any day now." The Collector has heard them all. If he catches you in a lie, then you can forget any possibility of setting up a payment schedule suitable to your needs.

Payment plans are not always readily agreed to. You'll have to convince the Collector of your sincerity in trying to resolve this debt. The first step is to sit down and talk to the Collector on friendly terms. Discuss *ALL* of your debts, and *ALL* of your income with him. Leave nothing unsaid. This is very important. It's your key to prove that you can't afford large payments. Show him, for instance, that your monthly income is $1681.97 and after mortgage, car, utilities, food, and gas expenses, you have a total of $157.14 left. This is your negotiating figure. You can't be left with nothing at all each month, so you might propose to make a monthly payment of 1/2 the remaining money. Paying $75 per month would be a very reasonable offer. The Collector will push for all of the remaining money, or at least $100 per month. Stand your ground, but don't get rude with him, or you won't come to an agreement at all. Listen to what he believes would be a fair payment arrangement, then calmly rationalize why the payments should be smaller.

Once a payment arrangement is agreed upon, put it in writing. Either have the Collector put it in writing and sign it, or you put it in writing (in complete detail) and send it in with your first payment. Most importantly, have him sign it and send it back to you. This is your proof that the arrangement was accepted. If he refuses to put it in writing, then ask him if it is all right to tape the conversation and payment arrangement. If he still refuses, he probably has something to hide. Is he looking for a way to get out of the agreement in the future? What if the account moves to another Collector (accounts frequently do). The new Collector might want to change the arrangements (they frequently do). They take the position that if you can pay $75 per month, then why not $100 per month. So have proof of your arrangements—get it in writing. PROTECT YOURSELF.

Not all payment arrangements are agreed upon. Many people send in payment arrangements without the agreement of the Collector. If this is done, then make payments large enough so as not to put yourself in trouble financially, and not small enough to make the Collector angry. Once you start payments (without an agreement), continue the payments on a regular schedule so the payments arrive in his office on the same day each month. After a few payments, the Collector will see, by the accuracy of each payment, that you mean business in settling the account. An important point to remember is that the Collector doesn't want to have to call you each month for a payment. He wants to get on with other accounts. Show him you are very dependable and chances are, he'll leave you alone. Remember what I said before—when you send a payment to a Collection Agency without a payment arrangement, make sure the amount of the check or Money Order is ample enough so as not to insult the Collector and make him angry. If you send $5, then don't be surprised if it's returned to you as unacceptable (rarely does this happen). Usually, they will just credit your account with it and call you up and argue about the amount of the check. If the check is accepted and cashed, then it *must* be applied to the account. Don't play games with them by sending $1 on a very large bill. The Collection Agency might decide to go to the Creditor and ask for the suit papers. Always make copies of all checks sent to the Agency. You'll never know when you'll need them.

If you believe your account will be placed with a Agency very shortly, then use this same information with the Creditor. Call them or go in and sit down with them and explain your situation and what you can do to better it. Remind them that it's better to accept your arrangements, than to turn it over to an Agency. This way they will get 100% of the money, and not have to pay a percentage to the Agency. This is both to your advantage and the Creditors'.

The following letter is an example of a possible payment arrangement proposal to the Collection Agency.

123 Cool Springs Drive
Wedgeton, Michigan 99939

Date

XYZ Collections   RE: The Jones Company
1 Park Street   ACCT #12345
Red Park, California 93777   Balance due : $500

Dear Mr. Green:

I apologize for the apparent disregard for the amount due to your Client, but I have truly suffered major financial difficulties in the past year. Obviously, I am in a position where I am having much trouble in meeting my monthly bills. This is why my account has been placed with your Agency. If I didn't care about my bill, I would not be writing this letter. I am hoping we can work out an arrangement that would be agreeable to both your Client and my financial situation.

First let me show you what my finances and bills look like. My income consists of 2 paychecks a month totaling $1600. I have no other income. That includes child support, Social Security checks or anything of the sort. I have only my paycheck from work. My monthly bills are as follows: mortgage $450, daycare $185, electric $65, gas $25, phone $49, food $300, car payment $265, car gas $40, insurance $65, medical bills $30, other credit cards $50. This is a grand total of $1524 in expenses per month. This leaves me $76. After analyzing my finances and income, I have come to the conclusion that I can offer $50 per month payment on my account to The Jone Company. This leaves $26 for myself in case I run short. I can't see how I can survive on $26 per month, but I will try to make do. If possible, I will try to save this $26 per month to hopefully accumulate enough to make an extra payment every other month. As you can see, I am trying my best to resolve this situation. Please consider my proposal of $50 per month as a good faith effort to eliminate my bill from your records.

Should you accept this proposal, then please communicate this through written correspondence at the address above. While I wait for your response, please accept the enclosed check for $50 as a good faith effort and the first check of many (with your acceptance).

Thank you in advance for your attention and cooperation. I look forward to resolving this matter.

Sincerely,
John Doe

As you can see, the Debtor asked him to respond to the above proposal in writing. The letter he sends back (accepting the payment arrangements), is my proof of acceptance. He cannot dispute it at a later date. I HAVE IT IN WRITING!

Offer A Settlement

There are times when you can pay off your bill earlier than you might think. Collection Agencies are sometimes authorized to accept a 75% settlement on the remaining balance, and sometimes more. This is strictly up to the Creditor. Make an offer and stand firm on that offer (unless you believe a settlement is not obtainable). Have the Collection Agency check with the Creditor to make sure a settlement is available, and for how much. It never hurts to ask. This could offer a tremendous savings. Negotiating with the Collector is your key to success. Negotiate for low payments or a settlement. This can definitely help you financially. The following 2 example letters might help you in accepting or obtaining a settlement.

123 Cool Springs Drive
Wedgeton, Michigan 99939

Date

XYZ Collections   RE: The Jones Company
1 Park Street   ACCT #12345
Red Park, California 93777   Balance due: $500

Dear Mr. Green:

Enclosed please find my check in the amount of $375 which represents 75% of the above balance due. On July 21, 1990, we spoke on the phone concerning my debt to The Jones Company. We came to an agreement that your Company would accept a check for 75% of the balance if it were paid all at once.

The back of the check has a restricted endorsement. It states: "This is to be accepted as a payment in full for account number 12345 with The Jones Company." Acceptance of this check constitutes payment in full. Your assistance in resolving this situation is greatly appreciated. If you have any questions, or have a problem with this check, then please don't hesitate to call me at home during the day.

Gratefully yours,
John Doe

123 Cool Springs Drive
Wedgeton, Michigan 99939

Date

XYZ Collections   RE: The Jones Company
#1 Park Street   ACCT # 12345
Red Park, California 93777   Balance due: $500

Dear Mr. Green:

I have spoken to you numerous times throughout the delinquency of my account, and we have not been able to agree upon a reasonable payment arrangement. So, I have spoken to a few of my relatives and have been able to scrape up some money, but not all of it. At this point I would like to make you an offer. If you can arrange it with your Client, I would be willing to settle the account with a check representing 75% of the balance. I realize you might be hesitant in accepting this offer, but I have made every reasonable effort possible to obtain as much of the money as I could. I cannot seem to scrape up another cent. I have truly suffered major financial difficulties in the last year, and cannot foresee additional funds coming in to help out in the near future. This offer is a good faith effort to resolve my financial obligation to The Jones Company.

If you accept this offer, then please communicate this through written correspondence at the address above. Thank you in advance for your attention and cooperation. I look forward to resolving this matter.

Sincerely,
John Doe

If you'll notice at the end of the letter, Mr. John Doe asked that the acceptance of this settlement be sent in writing. This is done so he has a letter from the Agency stating that they are accepting this settlement. This way, the Agency cannot come back later and demand the remaining balance of 25%. This protects your agreement.

Adding Expenses To The Bill

A Debt Collector may not use unfair or unconscionable means to collect or attempt to collect any debt. The following conduct is a violation of this section:

(1) The collection of any amount (including any interest, fee, charge, or expense incidental to the principal obligation), unless such amount is expressly authorized by the agreement creating the debt or permitted by law.

For purposes of this section, "amount" includes not only the debt, but also any incidental charges, such as collection charges, interest, service charges, late fees, and bad check handling charges.

LEGALITY OF CHARGES.

A Debt Collector may attempt to collect a fee or charge in addition to the debt if either (A) the charge is expressly provided for in the contract creating the debt and the charge is not prohibited by State law, or (B) the contract doesn't state it, but the charge is otherwise expressly permitted by State law. Stated another way, a Debt Collector may not collect an additional amount if either (A) State law expressly prohibits collection of the amount, or (B) the contract does not provide for collection of the amount and State laws say nothing about it. If State law permits collections of reasonable fees, the reasonableness and consequential legality of these fees is determined by State law.

AGREEMENT NOT IN WRITING.

A Debt Collector may establish an "agreement" without written contract. For example, he may collect a service charge on a dishonored check based on a posted sign on the merchant's premises allowing such a charge, if he can demonstrate that the Consumer knew of the charges.

(2) It is a violation to cause charges to be made to
     any person for communications by concealment
     of the true purpose of the communication. Such
     charges include, but are not limited to, collect
     telephone calls and telegram fees. An unscru-
     pulous Collector will call "collect" and claim it's
     an emergency. Usually the person will accept the
     charges thinking something horrible has hap-
     pened, and will soon come to find that it's just
     the Collector. This is an illegal tactic. But if the
     Consumer was aware that the call was from a
     Collection Agency and accepted the collect call,
     then the Consumer is liable for the charges
     incurred through this call.

Beware of added expenses. The only one who can add
interest or collection fees to the bill is the Creditor, not
the Collection Agency. When collection costs are added,
it is usually the amount that the Creditor had to pay the
agency to collect the bill.

It's In The Mail

Too many people lie, saying they will pay their bill. If you say you'll pay it, then *pay it.* If you are not going to pay the bill, then tell them so. Tell the truth. Lies just irritate the situation, and they have to call you back again and again. THEY WON'T GO AWAY.

COMMON LIES:
- It's in the mail.
- The stamp fell off the envelope.
- My letter to you was returned by the Post Office.
- I'm too busy to talk right now.
- I'll send it tomorrow.
- You should have gotten the check by now.
- I just sent it.
- I sent it yesterday.
- I forgot to mail it.
- I'm out of checks.
- I left it at work.
- I get paid tomorrow.
- I think my husband sent it.

Beware of promising to pay if you are unable to. If you promise to pay, they'll expect a check soon and will be calling back again and again to see where it is. Promising to pay only excites the Collector into calling again if they do not receive a check. If you promise to pay, then pay. Don't ask for more headaches by promising something you can't produce. Don't use these excuses as a stall tactic to give yourself more time to come up with the money. If you explain the circumstances and the fact that you need more time, and you're honest with him, he'll understand and give you the extra time you need.

Overnight Delivery

When a Bill Collector tells you to send it NEXT DAY AIR, or OVERNIGHT MAIL, then only do so if it is imperative that your money be there by a certain time to stop impending legal action. Your best bet is to send it REGISTERED or CERTIFIED with a return receipt requested. This will prove that it got there and ensures peace of mind. Now they cannot claim they have never received your check or money order. Your signed receipt from the recipient is your proof they have received your payment. Don't be coerced into spending extra money to get it there faster if it's not necessary. If you can't afford to pay the bill, then you probably can't afford the extra $10 to $14 to send it OVERNIGHT.

Postdated Checks

A Debt Collector may not use unfair or unconscionable means to collect or attempt to collect any debt. The following conduct is a violation:

(1) The acceptance by a Debt Collector from any person of a check or other payment instrument postdated by more than five days unless such person is notified in writing of the Debt Collector's intent to deposit such check or instrument not more than ten nor less than three business days prior to such deposit.

(2) The solicitation by a Debt Collector of any postdated check or other postdated payment instrument for the purpose of threatening or instituting criminal prosecution.

(3) Depositing or threatening to deposit any postdated check or other postdated payment instrument prior to the date on such check or instrument.

Beware of writing postdated checks. Postdated checks allow the Collector to obtain the money NOW and not have to worry about your account at a later date. They're all right if you anticipate having the money at a later date, but don't be convinced by the Collector that it is for your own good. If you write the check and date it for a later date next month, I suggest that you make sure the check clears the bank on the prescribed date. It's hard to cancel the check with the Agency (they are highly reluctant to do so), if you can't come up with the money. You can put a STOP PAYMENT on the check, but that costs you $10 to $20 of unnecessary costs, OR you can let the check "bounce" and get yourself into trouble with your bank. You can cause a lot of tension between you and the Collection Agency, in addition to the bounced check charges some agencies may charge you. Now, you are back to the same position, only now it costs you more to pay it off (bounced check fees at your bank). Writing a postdated check WILL benefit, if you WILL have the money on that date. If the check you postdated and sent to them is dated and received at least 5 days prior to the check being cashed, they must BY LAW send you a reminder notice stating that they are about to cash your check. It usually also states that if you have problems with this check clearing the bank, then you are to notify them immediately and straighten it out. THIS NOTIFICATION IS YOUR LEGAL RIGHT. Check your local State laws to see if postdated checks are acceptable.

Paid In Full

Paying off an account is only half the battle. You should protect yourself when you pay an account off. Write "PAID IN FULL" and the account number on the back of the check. They cannot come back and claim you owe more. Writing "paid in full" in the memo portion of the check does no good at all. Always write "paid in full" on the back of the check as close to the top as possible with your account number. When they endorse the check, they will sign under what you wrote and are accepting this check as paid in full. THIS PROTECTS YOU. Always request a PAID IN FULL receipt from the agency, and file it away.

Writing "paid in full" on your check does not protect you in all states. In 1989 the Ohio Supreme Court ruled that a Creditor can accept and cash a check marked "paid in full"as partial satisfaction of a debt and still pursue the Debtor for the balance by endorsing the check "UNDER PROTEST" or "WITHOUT PREJUDICE" or similar language which indicates that the Creditor is not accepting the check as payment in full. In other words, If a Creditor receives a check for less than the full balance marked "PAID IN FULL," he will add the words "UNDER PROTEST" or "WITHOUT PREJUDICE" to the endorsement. This protects the Creditor's right to pursue the remaining balance.

It is very important to protect yourself when paying off an account. Obtain a full release from the Creditor when writing "PAID IN FULL." This prevents them from coming back at a later date trying to pursue the remaining balance. Check your State Laws to see if this pertains to your situation.

Will A Creditor Sue?

How far will a Creditor go to get his money? This is a question many Debtors ask and fear. Will he write off your debt, send it to a Collector, or will he protect his legal rights to the money owed him? No one knows what the Creditor has on his mind. You *DO* owe the money, you *DID* sign a legal and binding contract, you are *NOT* repaying the debt according to the terms of your contract. He has a right to take this bill to court if he so desires, but will he? Let's first look at some important questions to ask yourself:

(1) HOW MUCH IS THE BILL?

(2) TO WHOM IS IT OWED?

(3) HOW LONG HAS IT BEEN DELINQUENT?

(4) DO YOU LIVE IN THE SAME STATE AS THE CREDITOR?

(5) ARE YOU AND YOUR CREDITOR ON SPEAKING TERMS?

(1) *HOW MUCH IS THE BILL?*

This is the most important question to look at. Costs to sue someone nowadays are so high that it is financially unfeasible for a Creditor to sue someone for $20, $50, or even $150. This does depend on the Creditor's willingness to go through with the suit. If they want to go through with the hassles of a Judgement, they can ask the courts that you pay for all costs involved in obtaining this Judgement. These costs could be court costs, filing fees, sheriff's and summons fees, and Attorney fees. If you read your contract, you'll probably find that you agreed to pay these additional costs.

If your bill is substantially higher, lets say $250 and more, your chances are greater of pending legal action. If your bill *is* substantially higher, you'll need to re-evaluate your financial situation and try to pay the bill as soon as possible, so as to avoid litigation. Creditors have more to gain by suing you if you have a large balance. Reviewing the next four questions might help ease your mind or show you what to consider if there might be possible legal action on the horizion.

(2) *TO WHOM IS IT OWED?*

How often has it been said "I'll sue you if I have to?" Is this company or individual willing to "go all the way?" I believe an INDIVIDUAL would have more to lose if you don't pay him, as opposed to a COMPANY. Two or three hundred dollars would be a bigger loss to an INDIVIDUAL than to a large company with a multi-million dollar a year income. Some COMPANIES might sue for as little as two or three hundred dollars, just to make a point or set an example. Suits for $500 and more are more common due to the size of the bill. No one can say that because it's $500 or more, you WILL be sued. It's still up to the Creditor, his policies, and how he sees your ability to pay the bill if a Judgement were obtained. Assess the amount of money you owe, to the probability of them suing to get it, to the probability of repaying it if a Judgement were obtained.

(3) *HOW LONG HAS IT BEEN DELINQUENT?*

If your account is 90 to 120 days past due, you still have time to work it out with the Creditor. Once your account goes past this point, it usually will be placed with a Collection Agency, and the Agency will try to work it out with you. If this can't be done, then they might recommend to the Creditor that a suit is in order. If the

Creditor believes that he'll *never* get the money from you, your chances are greater that he'll sue you to get it—depending on the amount owed.

(4) *DO YOU LIVE IN THE SAME STATE
     AS THE CREDITOR?*

Years ago, Debt Collectors would file suit against Consumers in courts which were so distant or inconvenient that the Consumers were unable to appear. As a result, the Debt Collectors obtained a Default Judgement, and the Consumer was denied his day in court. How could the Debtor win if he didn't show up for court? If you don't show, you can't defend yourself. Not all Creditors have an Attorney in the State where *YOU* live (if different from the Creditors), and sometimes they will just forget the possibility of suit. If you live in the *same* state as the Creditor, chances are he has an Attorney available to sue you.

A "FAIR VENUE" bill was passed which now protects the Debtor when he is being sued. A Debt Collector who files suit must do so either where the Consumer resides or where the contract was signed. When an action is against real property, the suit must be brought where this property is located.

Is the Creditor willing to go through with these "Fair Venue" standards to get his money? Do you OWN property? Again, is your bill large enough to warrant a suit?

(5) *ARE YOU AND THE CREDITOR
     ON SPEAKING TERMS?*

Should you still be on good terms with your Creditor, you should consider making acceptable terms to repay this debt. Sit down and speak with the Creditor and explain your situation. It can't hurt, but can only help. If you're not on speaking terms, then this could be to your disadvantage. If you make him angry enough or give him a reason to sue you, then you're only hurting yourself.

The last thing a Creditor wants to do is to turn your account over to an Agency. It will cost him usually anywhere between 8% and 60% in collection costs. He would much rather come to terms with you and be assured of 100% of the money.

A Judgement Against You

Many people claim that they are not able to pay, and if they have to go to court, then the Judge will rule in their favor. It's not as simple and as easy as that. For there to be a Judgement against you, the following must occur:

(1) You must be served with a summons and have notice of the Court date.

(2) Your case must be heard in Court. If you are not present, a Default Judgement (Judgement based only on one side—the side that is present) may be given against you. While in Court, you will be asked a few questions—probably something similar to this:

> (A) Is this your signature on the contract? (It is.)

> (B) Did you receive the product, services, or accept the loan? (You did.)

> (C) Are you paying back the bill or loan on time? (No, you are not.)

His final statement should be—GUILTY! He has ruled that you owe the money (you signed a legal and binding contract). The Judge usually will not set up a payment plan for you. That is between the Collection Agency and your Attorney. If the Agency refuses any payment arrangement, your Attorney can do nothing except argue your case. He can, however, state there is no way to pay the balance in full, and an arrangement is the only way they will get any money at all. Chances are, your Attorney and the Agency *will* come up

with a suitable arrangement. If no arrangement
can be made, then the Agency would probably
continue on with the suit. If a Judgement is
obtainied against you and you still do not pay,
you will be in CONTEMPT OF COURT!

Contacting a Consumer's employer prior to Judgement
can cause irreparable harm to the Consumer's job or
reputation and be disruptive to the Consumer's work
productivity. The Legislative Committee believes it is not
an employer's responsibility to collect debts for Debt
Collectors. Employers usually do not want to be contacted
by Debt Collectors. If a Consumer wants an employer's
help, the Consumer is fully able to request it. The Legislative
Committee strongly believes that a Debt Collector's contact
with a Consumer's employer prior to final Judgement
(absent Consumer consent or express Court permission)
constitutes an unwarranted invasion of the Consumer's
privacy and interference with Consumer's employee-
employer relationship.

Once there is a Judgement against you, the Creditor can
collect the Judgement by: (1) Having the sheriff seize and
sell your personal property (subject to certain property which
is exempt and varies from state to state). (2) Garnishment;
This is a Court order directing a third party, having your
property, to pay that property or a part thereof to the Creditor to satisfy the debt. There always must be a Judgement
against you before there can be a garnishment. They can
garnish your bank account (savings, checking, Credit Union,
etc.) if they know where the account is. They can garnish
your wages if they know where you work.

There is a Federal garnishment law which allows you
to retain a certain amount of your salary. The maximum

part of the aggregate earnings of any individual for any workweek, after the deduction from those earnings of any amount required by law to be withheld, which is subject to garnishment may not exceed (A) 25%, or (B) The amount by which his aggregate earnings for that week, after the deduction from those earnings of any amounts required to be withheld by law, exceed thirty times the Federal minimum hourly wage ($4.25/hr. × 30 hours = $100.50) whichever is less. In other words; the maximum part of the total disposable earnings of your paycheck for any work-week which is subjected to garnishment may not exceed 25% of your disposable earnings for that week, or the amount by which your disposable earnings for that week exceed 30 times the Federal minimun hourly wage ($4.25/hour). Whichever is less.

The term "GARNISHMENT" means any legal or equitable procedure through which the earnings of any individual are required to be withheld for payment of any debt.

The term "EARNINGS" means compensation paid, or payable for personal services, as wages, salary, commission, bonus, or otherwise, and includes periodic payment to a pension or retirement program.

Each state also sets limits on garnishments. Whichever (Federal or State) allows you to retain the most money is the one that applies. The states usually allow a head of household to retain more money. Some states allow RESIDENTS to retain more money than NON-RESIDENTS. Since this varies from state to state, you should check with a local Attorney to see what your state law provides. No employee shall be fired for reason of the fact that his earnings have been subjected to garnishment for any *one* indebtedness. *Some states* protect Consumers from discharge (being fired) based on the fact that they have several garnishments. The application of garnishment as a Creditor's remedy frequently results in loss of employment by the Debtor. The resulting disruption on employment, production, and consumption creates a substantial burden on our economic system nationwide.

WELFARE:

If you are on welfare, you may be what is called "Judgement proof." This means even if someone has a Judgement against you, they will have a difficult time trying to find something to collect. However, subject to certain property being exempt under state law, they can have the Sheriff seize and sell your personal property (car, jewelry, furniture, etc.). Depending on the type Judgement and the local state laws, a lien may be placed against any real estate you may own. They can also report your debt to a Creditor Bureau and you will have problems getting credit in the future.

BUSINESSES:

If your business is a SOLE PROPRIETORSHIP, you are treated as an individual. The fact that you have a business does not protect you. It only gives them more property (your business property) to seize and sell. If you pay yourself a salary, it can be garnished. If you are a sole proprietor and have a business bank account, it can be garnished.

BEING INCORPORATED:

If the incorporation is done correctly, you maintain all record keeping requirements, file all state corporation reports, etc., the corporation may shield your personal property. Even if you are incorporated, (unless you sign as an agent of the corporation and clearly indicate that you are not signing a contract as an individual), it is sometimes possible to be sued personally. *Corporations* can be sued. Judgements can be entered against them and they are subject to garnishment and seizure and sale of their property. Many banks will require the officers of a corporation to personally guarantee corporate debts.

DIVORCE DECREE:

Regardless of the stipulations of a DIVORCE DECREE, the original parties of the loan or revolving account are liable for repayment. They are contractual obligations, and will be reported as such.

Purchased Accounts

Some accounts are purchased by Agencies for pennies on the dollar. That means for every dollar owed on your account, the Agency paid FAR LESS than it's current value for the ownership of your account. EXAMPLE: If they paid 10¢ on the dollar and your bill was $100, then they paid $10 to buy your account. They now own your account. Any money paid on the account goes directly to the Agency. This does not affect the amount of the money owed on the account. Now the Agency can charge you interest on the account—only if the contract you signed states that interest can be charged. The Agency cannot change the terms of the contract. They MUST abide by the terms of the contract. The only difference is they OWN your account. This makes them not only the owner, but the FIRST PARTY. That means they are not a Collection Agency as far as YOUR account is concerned. They don't have to abide by most *Fair Debt Collection Practices Act* laws. They CAN apply minimal pressure to make you pay your bill. Remember, they must abide by the contract you signed, and they cannot raise your interest rates. Not all accounts placed with an Agency are purchased. Check your state laws on how far a FIRST PARTY can go to collect on an account.

Consumer Credit Counseling Services

If you are having debt problems, or are concerned about your financial situation, then *Consumer Credit Counseling Services* (CCCS) is your answer. The Counselors that work there are Professionals and have many of the answers to your problems. There are over 200 "NOT FOR PROFIT" community sponsored agencies across the United States. There are many more "PROFIT" agencies coast to coast. If they charge a fee, then how can they help your financial situation when you can't even afford to pay your bills as it is! Just call them for an appointment, and you will meet privately with one of their experienced Counselors who will analyze your current income, expenses, goals, and needs. They will then work out a budget hand-tailored to fit you. Your assets and debts will then be examined and possible solutions to your problems presented. If your situation is such that there is not enough money available to make full payments to your Creditors but enough for reasonable payments, you will be offered the option of going on their debt repayment plan. They will contact each Creditor on your behalf and make arrangements for them to accept reduced monthly payments. Your Creditors are then asked to stop all collection activity and to deal directly with CCCS. In some cases, Creditors will stop all finance charges to CCCS clients.

If you accept the debt repayment plan with CCCS, then each payday you would send payments to CCCS and they would send this money to your Creditors once a month. CCCS has the cooperation of many Creditors in the credit industry. Because of this cooperation, they may even be able to halt Judgements, repossessions, and get garnishments lifted. If there is not sufficient money available to set up a debt repayment plan through CCCS, your Counselor will work with you in deciding how your financial difficulties can best be handled. CCCS is dedicated to the education of the Consumer with financial problems. The ultimate answer to financial problems of most families lies in CCCS assistance *before* your accounts are placed with an Agency. CCCS Counselors are not Attorneys. Many people believe they *are* Attorneys representing their "CASE." Ask the CCCS if they have an ATTORNEY AT LAW in COLLECTIONS that they will recommend, if you need legal advise. If the Collection Agency does not accept CCCS's proposal (which they do not have to), then the Collector will continue with the Collection procedures.

Credit Cards

Today's society revolves around credit cards and the "instant credit" they contain. It's too easy to say "Charge it" and walk away with the merchandise in your hands. "I'll just take care of the bill when it arrives. In the mean time, that VCR is at its lowest price ever. Why wait till I have the cash, I've got my trusty credit card." Don't be carried away by the abundance of goods and the ease with which the magic words "charge it" are uttered. Everything you buy must be paid for, so use your credit wisely. Shop as carefully when you buy on credit as when you pay cash. Don't abuse charge privileges by buying thoughtlessly. Once you get behind in your payments, it is difficult to catch up. Then, in no time your account has been placed with a Collection Agency. If you cannot make your payments, take the initiative in explaining the situation to the credit department of the store before any payment is overdue. Remember that you have a limit on all of your accounts and you have a contractual obligation to stay within that limit. Your history of payment on your charge account will become a permanent part of your credit record. So make all of your charge account payments on time. If you have charge accounts at more than one store, keep a close check on your total credit purchases so that you will be able to meet all of your payments when due.

The term "CREDIT" means any card, plate, coupon book or other credit device existing for the purpose of obtaining money, property, labor, or services on credit.

The term "CARD HOLDER" means any person to whom a credit card is issued, or any person who has agreed with the card issuer to pay obligations arising from the issuance of a credit card to another person.

The term "UNAUTHORIZED USE" means a use of a credit card by a person other than the card holder who does not have actual, implied, or apparent authority for such use and from which the card holder receives no benefit.

Making the scheduled payment is one thing, but what if you have a dispute on the charges you have incurred? An unauthorized person could have used your card, there could be a dispute of the charges on the statement, or your card was stolen. These problems occur more often than you could imagine. There is a law which protects the Consumer's interest in the case of an error or complaint with respect to a billing statement called the FAIR CREDIT BILLING ACT (FCBA). To protect your RIGHTS under the FCBA when a billing error is suspected, you must write to the Creditor within 60 days to lodge the complaint of error. Once the error has been reported, you can withhold payment on ONLY THE AMOUNT OF THE ERROR. The Creditor is obligated also to remove finance charges assessed on the amount in question.

If there is a billing error on your credit card statement, the credit card company must send a written explanation or clarification to you, the reason why the Creditor believes your account was correctly shown in the statement, and upon request provide copies of evidence of the indebtedness. In the case of a billing error where the Debtor claims that the statement reflects goods not delivered to the Debtor, the Creditor may not construe such amount to be correctly shown unles he determines that such goods were actually delivered or mailed, and provides the Debtor with a statement of such determination. After the Creditor provides proof of above, the Creditor has no further responsibility of proof if the Debtor continues to make the same allegation about the same error.

If a Creditor receives a further written notice from a Debtor that an amount is still in dispute, a Creditor may not report to any third party or Credit Bureau that the amount is delinquent because the Consumer has failed to pay that is, unless the Creditor also reports that the amount is in dispute. After receiving a notice from the Consumer, a Creditor may not directly or indirectly threaten to report to any person adversely on the Consumer's credit rating or credit standing because of the Consumer's failure to pay the amount indicated by the Creditor? In addition, such amount may not be reported as delinquent to any third party or Credit Bureau until the Creditor has allowed the Consumer not less than 10 days to make payment. If a Creditor declares a complaint unjustified, its billing office must advise the local Credit Bureau of the FCBA dispute. When an FCBA dispute is reported to a Credit Bureau by a Creditor, the Consumer has the right to place a written statement giving the Consumer's side of the dispute in his or her Credit Bureau file.

If the card holder was under *NO* compulsion by fraud, duress, or otherwise voluntarily permitted the use of his or her credit card by another person, then the card holder AUTHORIZED the use of that card and is thereby responsible for any charges as a result of that use. This is true even if he orally requested that the other person not charge over a certain amount. In any action by a card issuer to enforce liability for the use of a credit card, the burden of proof is upon the card issuer to show that the use was authorized. The card holder is LIABLE ONLY for the unauthorized use UP TO $50.

Whoever knowingly uses, attempts, or conspires to use any counterfeit, fictitious, altered, forged, lost, stolen, or fraudulently obtained credit card to obtain money, goods, services, or anything else of value which within any one year period has a value totaling $1,000 or more, shall be fined not more than $10,000 or imprisoned not more than 10 years, OR BOTH!

As you can see, not only does the *Fair Debt Collection Practices Act* protect you from Bill Collectors, but the *Fair Debt Collection Practices Act* protects you from credit card disputes and unauthorized uses by other persons.

Sample Dispute Letter

123 Cool Springs Drive
Wedgeton, Michigan 99939

Date

Credit Card Company   RE: The Jones Company
2001 Harvest Time Street   ACCT #67890
Grapevine, Ohio 40608   Disputed Balance: $495.00

To Whom It May Concern:

On April 3, 1990, I purchased a lawn mower with my credit card from The Jones Company. The price of $495 is the exact (disputed) figure as shown on my statement. This lawn mower was on sale for a special price on television. I phoned in my order on their 800 number. They said my order would be delivered in 4 weeks. My purchase was to be delivered by UPS. Six weeks went by and I still did not receive my mower. I called the 800 number again and they did claim it was delivered in 4 weeks as promised. It has now been 8 weeks and my new mower still has not arrived. I see no need to pay my bill, if I have never received it. The people who sent the mower to me claim they have my signature on the delivery slip. The signature they have on the slip has to be someone else's. They must have delivered it to the wrong address. It is not my job to prove that I *didn't* receive it. It is your job to prove that I *did* receive it. Until this proof is provided, this charge will remain in dispute or will be removed from my credit card.

Please contact me at the address below if you receive any information on the whereabouts of my lawn mower, or any additional information on my dispute. Thank your for your time and consideration.

Sincerely,
John Doe

This is just a sample letter of a dispute with a charge card company. It is up to the credit card company to prove that you do owe the money. Be prepared to back your dispute with facts. For instance, if this Consumer can obtain a copy of the delivery slip, he can show that the signature is not his.

Bankruptcy, A Way Out?

Bankruptcy is a very serious step many Debtors take to avoid the possible repossession of their car, home, and furniture. Sometimes it is the *only* way to protect your possessions. Obviously, your credit rating is already in trouble, and Bill Collectors are "hounding" you day and night. Not only do the Collectors call you at work, but they are jeopardizing your job. Bills are pouring in and your paycheck just won't stretch that far. The final clincher is when your lender is threatening to foreclose on your home mortgage. Is there any way out?

Federal law provides one last possible answer: BANK-RUPTCY! When your debts exceed your assests, the legal system allows you to file a bankruptcy petition in Federal Court, designed to provide protection from your Creditors.

There are *two* kinds of bankruptcy available—Chapter 7 and Chapter 13. In Chapter 7, the Debtor's assets are used to pay the Creditors and bankruptcy expenses. Debts that cannot be repaid from your assets will be canceled or discharged. In Chapter 13, the Debtor develops a plan to repay his Creditors with usually smaller payments over a longer period of time.

CHAPTER 7:

What happens when you file a Chapter 7 bankruptcy petition? First, Bill Collectors and Creditors *must* stop calling and writing you to get you to pay your bills. They only know to stop calling and writing, when you or your Attorney notifies them of your intentions. All lawsuits dealing with your Creditors, including foreclosure of your home, are put to a SUDDEN HALT. Your assets and debts are then listed with your Attorney. This is where your Attorney earns his money. His first concern is saving your home.

Your home—to lose it, or not to lose it.

That is the question. Remember the morgage papers you signed? These papers give the lender the right to foreclose on your home, whether you file for bankruptcy or not. The reason: your mortgage lender is a "SECURED CREDI-TOR." The lender will decide whether or not to force you to sell your home. This will depend on how far you are behind on your payments and your ability to catch up. If you are only five or six payments behind, you have a good chance of coming to an agreement with the lender on an easy repayment plan. If you are behind eight or nine payments, then you can usually count on losing your home to a forced sale. But then,who's to say. It's up to the Creditor.

A forced sale of your home will leave you with *some* money. The law allows you to keep $5,000 ($10,000 for married couples) of equity in a home (the value over and above the mortgage). What happens to the rest of the money if you have more than $5,000 ($10,000 if married) equity in your home? The following example will explain. If, for instance, your home is worth $75,000, and the first mortgage is $40,000, a second mortgage of $15,000 lowers your equity in the home to $20,000, *but*, you are only allowed to keep $5,000 ($10,000 if married). If you owed $15,000 or more to your Creditors, then the house still might have to be sold. The $75,000 from the sale of the home would first be used to pay your mortgages of $55,000. The next $5,000 (or $10,000) would be yours, and the remaining $10,000 or $15,000 would be used to pay other Creditors. What if your mortgage is discharged? As a final example, if the value of your home is $75,000, and your mortgages total $70,000, then the sale of your home might not be necessary—because after the mortgages were paid and *your* $5,000 protected, nothing would be left for other Creditors.

CHAPTER 13:

Under Chapter 13, the Debtor can come up with a plan to pay back "SECURED CREDITORS" within a three to five year period (with approval from Court). This plan also allows you to repay your unsecured Creditors at least what they would have received if you filed Chapter 7. With a steady job, Chapter 13 would possibly be your best bet. It would allow you more time to catch up on your past due bills, and most importantly, time to catch up on your past due house payments and save your home. With a Chapter 13, you *must* pay all of your current obligations, and a portion of your earnings must also go towards catching up on the past due amounts.

Is bankruptcy really the answer? Bankruptcy can severly damage your credit record. It does not wipe your credit slate clean and give you a "fresh start." This remains on your Credit Bureau Report for ten years. Chapter 13 is usually less devastating than a Chapter 7, because at least you are making an attempt to pay back your Creditors. When all else fails, bankruptcy might be your only choice. However, it's not going to make it easy to get future loans. Within a few years of declaring bankruptcy and reestablishing your credit worthiness, you may qualify for FHA loan approval. When *some* lending and credit card companies find out that you have declared Chapter 7 bankruptcy, they are eager to give you loans and credit cards. Why? You have no more obligations to other companies and you should have no problems paying back your "new obligations." They know you can't file bankruptcy again for many years. On the other hand, you'll have trouble getting the credit you really need: a car, home, credit cards, education, personal needs, etc. If you doubt this, then contact any Creditor. Most Creditors are reluctant and seldom extend credit to someone who has filed for bankruptcy. That's true whether you file for straight bankruptcy under Chapter 7 or if you file under Chapter 13 with the intention of repaying your debts. Don't fall into the trap you have just escaped. Resist the new temptation and just try to get your life back into shape. Before you consider bankruptcy, contact your Creditors first. Try to work out a payment plan with them. Remember they want to see you solve your financial problems just as much as you do. So before you make a ten-year bankruptcy decision, think. Consider the alternatives and don't lock yourself into bankruptcy unnecessarily.

5

Location Information

Locating the Consumer through
Reports and Applications

Credit Application Information

Applications you fill out for loans, credit, apartment rental, etc. are used to locate you if you skip out on your debt or you're just not paying anymore. Most credit applicants believe the information they have disclosed on their application is private information and only available to the company to which they have applied for credit. It IS common practice for different Creditors to call each other to compare records and application information on an individual. This is usually only done when you have defaulted on a loan with Company "A," and it is necessary for them to call Company "B" to get new information on locating you. The Federal Trade Commission states that a Debt Collector (when obtaining location information) may not refer to the Consumer's Debts in any third party communication, including those with other Creditors. The Collector can call to get location information, but cannot state that you owe a debt. Although the *Fair Debt Collection Practices Act* generally protects the Consumer's privacy by limiting Debt Collector communications about personal affairs to third parties, it recognizes the need for some third party contact by Collectors to seek the whereabouts of the Consumer.

Typical items used to locate you on your application are: Social Security number, references (friends and relatives), former jobs, previous addresses, bank accounts, driver's license number, neighbors, and other Creditors. Once a Debt Collector learns a Consumer is represented by an Attorney, he must limit his request for location information to the Attorney.

Be careful when listing a Creditor as a reference. If you list a BAD CREDITOR (one that you stopped paying, are late on your payments, or are "running from"), he is more likely to divulge some bad information about you. For instance, if a Creditor is looking for you and he calls a

"Bad Creditor," the bad Creditor is very likely to give him all of the information he has in order to locate you, including home and work numbers. As opposed to the "Bad Creditors," the "Good Creditor" will help your situation. He is less likely to divulge information on your whereabouts or how to locate you. As a former Bill Collector, I found that a "Good Creditor" is usually hesitant to give out information concerning you. Perhaps he believes that if you are not paying someone else and he finally locates you and sues to get the money, this would jeopardize the money you are paying him. He would not want to jeopardize your credit with him. Simply, the "Bad Creditor" has nothing to lose by giving out information on you (you are not paying him anyway), but the "Good Creditor" has *everything* to lose. So long as you are in good standing with him, then why should he cause problems? Friends, relatives, and neighbors used as references work the same way. If you are at odds with one of them, I would suggest *not* using him or her as a reference. The "ultimate revenge" against you would be to give a Creditor damaging information about your credit, background, or character.

Now what do you do? Credit was NOT extended to you. For some reason or another, you thought this loan was important, or you would not have applied for it. Don't "burn your bridges" behind you. Stay in good relations with your Creditors, friends, relatives, and neighbors. They can hurt you as well as help you. Most of all, keep *all* of your obligations to Creditors up-to-date and on time. You won't have to worry about whom to list as a Credit reference if you are on good terms with everyone. A credit application is a waste of time if you have poor credit history and references.

Credit Bureau Reports

For the benefit of this section, the terms "CONSUMER REPORT" or "CREDIT BUREAU REPORT" mean any written, oral, or other communication of any information by a Consumer Reporting Agency bearing on a Consumer's credit worthiness, credit standing, or credit capacity, which is used or expected to be used for credit purposes.

The term "CONSUMER REPORTING AGENCY" means any organization which, for monetary fees, dues, or on a non-profit basis, regularly engages in the practice of assembling or evaluating Consumer credit information or other information on Consumers for the purpose of furnishing Consumer Reports to third parties.

Before credit is extended to you, most Creditors want to know your credit history. This information is obtained from two sources—the Credit Bureau Report, and the credit application you have just completed. Credit Bureaus are computer companies which collect and store information about your credit history. Your credit file is an accumulation of information on how you pay your bills and is used as a guide to determine if you are a good credit risk.

Credit Bureaus do not evaluate your "credit worthiness." The Creditor decides this, based on their own policies and standards. These standards can vary from Creditor to Creditor. What they look at is how current your payments are, how easily you pay off an account, and your ability and willingness to comply with the terms of your obligations. After reading your credit history, the Creditor then will decide if they wish to extend credit to you. Not all Creditors report your credit information to a Credit Bureau, so there will be times when you'll notice that your report is incomplete. This is up to the Creditor if he wishes to report your information. Creditors may choose to verify additional credit references that you have listed on your application that are not on your Credit Bureau Report, by contacting them directly.

The banking system is dependent upon fair and accurate credit reporting. Inaccurate credit reports directly impair the efficiency of the banking system, and unfair credit reporting methods undermine the public confidence which is essential to the continued functioning of the banking system. Without accurate reporting, a Credit Bureau is useless to the Creditor. Consumer Reporting Agencies have assumed a vital role in assembling and evaluating Consumer credit and other information on Consumers. It is necessary to insure that Consumer Reporting Agencies exercise their grave responsibilities with fairness, impartiality, and a respect for the Consumer's right to privacy. Whenever these agencies prepare a Consumer report, they are to follow reasonable procedures to assure maximum possible accuracy of the information concerning the individual about whom the report relates. The Agency cannot alter information reported to them in any way.

Permissible Purposes Of Consumer Reports

A Consumer Reporting Agency may furnish a Consumer Report under the following circumstances:

(1) in response to the order of a Court having jurisdiction to issue such an order;

(2) in accordance with the written instructions of the Consumer to whom it relates;

(3) to a person to which it has reason to believe—
   (A) intends to use the information in connection with a credit transaction involving the Consumer on whom the information is to be furnished and involving the extension of credit to, or review, or collection of an account of the Consumer;

   (B) intends to use the information for employment purposes; or

   (C) otherwise has a legitimate business need for the information in connection with a business transaction involving the Consumer.

Not only can a Creditor request a Credit Bureau Report on the Consumer, but the Consumer can request that a report be pulled on himself (there will be a fee for this report. Ask the Agency for their schedule of fees.)

Credit Bureau disclosures will be made to the Consumer *in person* if he furnishes proper identification, or by telephone if he has made a written request with proper identification. You will be permitted to be accompanied by one other person of your choosing, who shall furnish reasonable identification. A Consumer Reporting Agency may require you to furnish a written statement granting permission to the Consumer Reporting Agency to discuss your file in this person's presence. Every Consumer Reporting Agency will, upon request and proper identification of the Consumer, clearly and accurately disclose to the Consumer:

(1) the nature and substance of all information in its files on the Consumer at the time of the request;

(2) the sources of the information; and

(3) the recipients of your report.

The Agency will provide trained personnel to explain to you any information furnished, and will make the disclosures only during normal business hours and on reasonable notice.

Items that must be removed from the Credit Bureau Report are:

- Bankruptcy—after ten years.

- Judgements—after seven years (or when the statute of limitations expires, whichever is longer).

- Paid tax liens—after seven years.

- Collection accounts or those charged with profit and loss-after seven years.

- Arrests, indictments, or convictions—after seven years.

- Any other adverse item of information—after seven years.

Some Creditors or Collection Agencies report information on a Credit Bureau Report about your delinquency, to catch you in the future—you probably won't get the new loan you are applying for until you pay off your delinquent bill. This usually works rather well.

The following are examples of information contained in a Credit Bureau Report:

- your Social Security number
- date of birth
- current address and previous address
- current phone number
- your spouse's name and Social Security number

- current employer and address
- your position
- date hired
- date information was reported
- date you were terminated from your job

- previous employer and address
- spouse's employment information
- names of your Creditors
- date accounts were opened
- high credit on the account (highest amount ever owed)

- balance you owe to the Creditor
- amount past due
- payment pattern (whether payments are late or on time)

- type of account (revolving, installment, mortgage, etc.)

- number of payments
- dollar amount and frequency of each payment
- the account number
- credit limit
- date the account was closed

- who is responsible for paying the account
- the collateral used for the installment loan
- type of installment loan (automobile, boat, personal, etc.)
- if the account is in dispute
- the amount your account is delinquent
- the number of times the account has been (30, 60, 90, 120 days) delinquent

- Public information (Judgements against you and from whom)

As you can see, Credit Bureau Agencies try to leave nothing untouched. Now you should understand why a Credit Bureau Report is so important to a potential Creditor. He wants to see exactly how your finances are doing, and whether or not you will be a "credit risk."

Credit Bureau Reports are used by Collection Agencies on a regular basis. With this report, a Collection Agency can locate a person's new place of employment or a new address. If this report still does not supply enough information about a person, then they might try calling one of your other Creditors and exchange information on you (past and present) to update their records.

Consumer Reporting Agencies require that prospective users of the information identify themselves, clarify the purpose for which the information is sought, and certify that the information will be used for no other purpose. Every Consumer Reporting Agency shall make a reasonable effort to verify the identity of a new prospective user and the uses certified by such prospective user prior to furnishing such user a Consumer Report.

Procedure In Case Of Disputed Accuracy

If the completeness or accuracy of any item of information contained in your file is disputed, and the dispute is directly conveyed to the Consumer Reporting Agency, that Agency will (within a reasonable period of time) reinvestigate and record the current status of that information unless it has reasonable grounds to believe that the dispute is frivolous or irrelevant. If, after the reinvestigation, the information is found to be inaccurate or can no longer be verified, the Agency will promptly delete the information. The presence of contradictory information in your file does not in and of itself constitute reasonable grounds for believing the dispute is frivolous or irrelevant.

If the reinvestigation does not resolve the dispute, you may file a brief statement setting forth the nature of your dispute. The Agency may limit the statements to not more than one hundred words. They will provide you with assistance in writing a clear summary of the dispute. Whenever a statement of a dispute is filed, unless there is reasonable grounds to believe that it is frivolous or irrelevant, the Agency will, in any subsequent Consumer Report containing the information in question, clearly state that it is disputed by you and provide either your statement or a clear and accurate summary.

Following any deletion of information which is found to be inaccurate, or any notation as to disputed information, the Consumer Reporting Agency will, at your request, furnish notification that the item has been deleted to any person specifically designated by you who received a Consumer Report which contained the deleted or disputed information.

Any Consumer Reporting Agency or *user* of information which willfully fails to comply with Federal guidelines with respect to any Consumer is liable to that Consumer in an amount equal to the sum of:

(1) any actual damages sustained by the Consumer as a result of the failure;

(2) such amount of punitive damages as the Court may allow; and

(3) in the case of any successful action to enforce any liability, the costs of the action together with reasonable Attorney fees as determined by the Court.

An action to enforce any liability created, may be brought in any appropriate United States District Court, or in any other Court of competent jurisdiction, within two years from the date on which the liability arises.

Any person who knowingly and willfully obtains information on a Consumer from a Consumer Reporting Agency under false pretenses shall be fined not more than $5000 or imprisoned not more than one year or both. Any officer or employee of a Consumer Reporting Agency who knowingly and willfully provides information concerning an individual from the Agency's files to a person not authorized to receive that information shall be fined not more than $5000 or imprisoned not more than one year or both.

No consumer may bring any action or proceeding in the nature of defamation, invasion of privacy, or negligence with respect to the reporting of information against any Consumer Reporting Agency, any user of information, or any person who furnishes information to a Consumer Reporting Agency, except if false information is furnished with malice or willful intent to injure the Consumer.

If a Debt Collector knows that a debt is disputed by the Consumer, either from a receipt of written notice or other means, and reports it to a Credit Bureau, he must report it as disputed. When a Debt Collector learns of a dispute *after* reporting the debt to a Credit Bureau, the dispute should also be reported.

As you can see, this is a very valuable report. A car or house loan can depend on this report. If you stop paying bills, then they stop giving loans. Many people claim that they don't care what happens to their rating on a Credit Bureau Report. Let's be honest. Life revolves around this report. You'll buy another car someday, a TV, stereo, furniture, etc. You *will* use credit again, so don't ruin your credit by out and out *not* paying your bills. Think of the "Great American Dream"—OWNING A HOME. You are putting it further and further from your reach.

The following is a sample letter to a Credit Reporting Agency:

123 Cool Springs Drive
Wedgeton, Michigan 99939

Date

Consumer Reporting Agency	RE: Auto Repair Center
1694 Praise Ave.	ACCT # 45678
Eternity City, NH 43435	Disputed balance: $400

To whom it may concern:

Recently I applied for credit at my local bank and was turned down due to a discrepancy on my Credit Bureau Report. I have had only one problem with my credit, and that was with the Auto Repair Center. I drove my '88

Oldsmobile to their center on July 21, 1990, and stated that I needed an all-around brake job. The job entailed putting brake shoes on the rear, and pads on the front. Steve (the brake man) filled out the order form just as I had requested the work to be done. Nothing else was written on the form. He asked that I sign the order, which I did. He said the car would be ready in two hours, so I went shopping. Upon my return, I was handed a bill for $700. I was shocked to see that they not only repaired my brakes, but put four new tires on my car. I *did not* request tires to be put on my car. They put them on without my consent. I asked them to remove them from my car and they refused. We must have argued for an hour. The only way I could get my car back was to put this bill on my charge card. As soon as I received my credit card statement, I refused to pay it because I didn't order the tires. They then turned the account over to a Collection Agency. I wrote them a letter disputing the charges (this was my right per the *Fair Debt Collection Practices Act)*. I wrote them a check for the brake repair which I ordered. The remaining $400 for the new tires was not paid. I sent a dispute letter to the credit card company, the Collection Agency, and now to you. I am asking that you document this dispute on my Credit Bureau Report and send a copy of this letter along with the documentation of my dispute to my bank. Their address is: BANKS ARE US, 121 Money Circle, Smithville CA 97759. As I told the Collection Agency, until you can prove that I owe this debt, I refuse to pay it.

If you need additional information or have any questions, please contact me at the address above.

Sincerely,
John Doe

This sample letter tried to give as much information as the Consumer could remember. If you need to write a letter to the Credit Reporting Agency, then try to be as accurate and complete as possible. Don't be afraid to include too much information. The more complete the letter, the better off you will be.

Social Security Reports

Your Social Security number is an important tool for a Collection Agency. Collection Agencies subscribe to a service (for a fee) from the Credit Reporting Agencies, which allows them to enter your Social Security number into their computer. In turn, this computer gives them a printout of some very helpful and important information—your current and former addresses. This report is used to update your current address, if they do not have it at the time. If you move without a forwarding address, then this will certainly help them find you. Not all reports show your *current* address. Some just show your *last reported address.* This is still helpful to the Collectors. This address allows them to contact former employers and inquire as to your whereabouts and your place of employment. Remember the old cliche': YOU CAN RUN, BUT YOU CAN'T HIDE! (It's sad but true). It is almost impossible to go through life without using your Social Security number one time or another. Each time your number is used, you are updating your address files. These Social Security reports are *not* associated with the Government or the Social Security Administration. These inquiries are not considered an invasion of privacy, nor are they illegal.

City Directory

A City Directory is a publication showing addresses and phone numbers by streets in alphabetical order. They are available at libraries and for purchase to Collection Agencies. These books are divided into two sections:

SECTION 1.

It is used by looking up someone's address and getting a phone number to it, (if not supplied on your application, or the phone number is listed under someone else's name). If no number is provided in the City Directory, then there are phone numbers of neighbors to call and leave messages for the person they are searching for. While talking to a neighbor, they will ask questions like: Do you know them? What is their phone number? Where do they work? What time will they be home? This information they are requesting is called "location information." When a Collector tries to obtain location information, this may only cover Debtor's residential address, home phone number, and *place* of employment. It does not cover work phone numbers, names of Supervisors and their telephone numbers, salaries, or dates of paydays.

SECTION 2.

This section is strictly phone numbers. Look up the phone number, and it will tell you who lives there and their address. Even a telephone book gives them information on locating you. It tells them your address and telephone number. If you have an odd name, then there will be less names to choose from. The chances are very likely for them to call all of the similar names of a specified name and run across a relative of yours. From them they can get all the information they want about you (if the party is willing). There is not much you can do to hide from a Bill Collector. They know the game and how to play it.

6

Suing An Agency

Suing a Collection Agency is very difficult. You must provide proof of your LEGAL RIGHTS being violated. Show proof of this wrong-doing by a legally obtained recording of the conversation between you and the Collector, an illegal letter they sent you, or a witness. Always keep a detailed record of dates, places, times, and witnesses to the illegal action. Once you have proof of an illegal act by a Collection Agency, contact an Attorney. If you cannot afford an Attorney, contact the Federal Trade Commission or the Attorney General in your State. They will help clear up the discrepancies or will investigate the situation and take whatever actions are necessary to resolve or correct the problem.

Any Debt Collector who fails to comply with the *Fair Debt Collection Practices Act* is liable to the Debtor in an amount equal to the sum of the actual damage sustained by the Debtor as a result of the failure. The courts have awarded "actual damages" for *Fair Debt Collection Practices Act* violations that were not just out-of-pocket expenses, but included damages for personal humiliation, embarrassment, mental anguish, or emotional stress. In the case of any illegal action by an individual Collector, the damages may not exceed $1,000. The courts may fine the Collection Agency many more thousands of dollars, depending on the findings of the Courts. In determining the amount of liability for the illegal action, the Court will consider:

(1) the frequency and persistence of the illegal action by the Debt Collector,

(2) if his actions were intentional,

(3) if any third parties were involved,

(4) copies of illegal letters sent to the Consumer,

(5) a legally obtained recording of the illegal conversation,

(6) and witnesses to the illegal action.

The Debt Collector will *not* be held liable in any suit brought against him, if he can prove that the violation was not intentional and resulted from a bona fide error. He must also show that everything in his power was done to avoid the error by following the rules set forth in the *Fair Debt Collection Practices Act.*

Be careful when suing an Agency. It is your job to prove that they committed an illegal action. If a suit is brought in bad faith against the Collection Agency for the purpose of harassing the Agency, the Courts may award the Collection Agency Attorney's fees (reasonable in relation to the work expended and costs).

A lawsuit may be brought into any appropriate United States District Court, or in any Court of competent jurisdiction, within one year from the date on which the violation occurs. This can be done without regard to the size or delinquency of your bill.

INCIDENT REPORT

Name of Collection Agency _____

Address of Agency _____

_____

Name of Bill Collector _____

Other Person/Persons Involved _____

_____

Date/Dates of Occurrence _____

Event Which Took Place _____

_____

_____

_____

_____

_____

_____

_____

Witnesses _____

Location Incident Took Place _____

_____

Law Which Was Broken _____

_____

Collection Agency's Phone Number _____

Collection Agency's Supervisor _____

Closing Statement

I hope this book has cleared up any questions you had about Collection Agencies, illegal tactics used, what to do when they call, and the law as stated per the *Fair Debt Collection Practices Act*. Now that you are familiar with the law, maybe we can put an end to the unscrupulous Collector, and his illegal and harassing techniques in obtaining money. Remember, there are a lot of good Collectors out there, and they are just doing their job. Without these people, you would have to pay at least DOUBLE for everything you buy. Let's not close these Agencies—just put them back on the right path. You should not fear Collection Agencies, but be willing to work with them to resolve your financial disposition.

Now that you are armed, Collection Agencies will respect you more and get down to the business at hand. They would not dare break the law, knowing you know as much about the law as they do. Remember the "KEY" to successful negotiations—don't make the Creditor or Collector angry or he will not accept your proposals. His job is to take *control* of the situation. Now, who really has control?

If you have any questions that go beyond the information provided to you, then please seek expert professional assistance through an Attorney, the Federal Trade Commission, or the Attorney General in your State.

If you would like to read verbatim what the law says about the *Fair Debt Collection Practices Act*, this information follows immediately. It is taken straight from the Federal law books, and is helpful in obtaining exact wording of the law as it was passed in 1977.

Federal Legislation

FAIR DEBT COLLECTION PRACTICES ACT

(Also known as *Consumer Credit Protection Act*)

Dates of consideration and passage:

House—April 4 and September 8, 1977
Senate—August 5, 1977

The Senate report is set out.

Senate Report No. 95-382

The Committee on Banking, Housing, and Urban Affairs, to which was referred the bill (H.R. 5294) to amend the Consumer Credit Protection Act to prohibit abuses by Debt Collectors, having considered same, reports favorable thereon with an amendment and recommends that the bill as amended do pass.

History Of The Legislation

On May 12 and 13, 1977, the Consumer Affairs Subcommittee held hearings on four bills to regulate debt collection practices:

   (1) S.656—introduced by Senator Biden;

   (2) S.918—introduced by Senator Riegle;

   (3) S.1130—introduced by Senator Garn for himself and Senators Schmitt and Tower;

   (4) H.R.5294—passed by the House of Representatives on April 4, 1977.

After these hearings and before markup by the committee, Senator Riegle offered a composite bill, designated Committee Print No. 1, with amendments, by voice vote. The committeee substituted the text of its bill for that of H.R.5294, which is herewith reported without objection.

Nature And Purpose Of The Bill

This legislation would add a new title to the Consumer Protection Act entitled the FAIR DEBT COLLECTION PRACTICES ACT. Its purpose is to protect Consumers from a host of unfair, harassing, and deceptive debt collection practices without imposing unnecessary restrictions on ethical Debt Collectors. This bill was strongly supported by consumer groups, labor unions, State and Federal law enforcement officials, and by both national organizations which represent the debt collection profession, the American Collectors Association, and Associated Credit Bureaus.

Need For This Legislation

The committee has found that Debt Collection abuse by third party Debt Collectors is a widespread and serious national problem. Collection abuse takes many forms, including obscene or profane language, threats of violence, telephone calls at unreasonable hours, misrepresentation of a Consumer's rights, disclosing a Consumer's personal affairs to friends, neighbors, or an employer, obtaining information about a Consumer through false pretense, impersonating public officials and Attorneys, and simulating legal process.

Debt collection by third parties is a substantial business which touches the lives of many Americans. There are more than 5,000 Collection Agencies across the country, each averaging eight employees. Last year (1978) more than $5 billion in debts were turned over to Collection Agencies. One trade association which represents approximately half of the nation's independent Collectors states that in 1976 its members contacted eight million Consumers.

Hearings before the Consumer Affairs Subcommittee revealed that independent Debt Collectors are the prime source of egregious collection practices. While unscrupulous Debt Collectors comprise only a small segment of the industry, the suffering and anguish which they regularly inflict is substantial. Unlike Creditors, who generally are restrained by the desire to protect their good will when collecting past due accounts, independent collectors are likely to have no future contact with the Consumer and often are unconcerned with the Consumer's opinion of them. Collection Agencies generally operate on a 50% commission, and this has too often created the incentive to collect by any means.

The primary reason why Debt Collection abuse is so widespread is the lack of meaningful legislation on the State level. While Debt Collection Agencies have existed for decades, there are 14 States, with forty million citizens, that have no debt collection laws. These States are: Alabama, Delaware, Georgia, Kansas, Kentucky, Mississippi, Missouri, Montana, Ohio, Oklahoma, Rhode Island, South Carolina, South Dakota, and Virginia. Another eleven States (Alaska, Arkansas, Indiana, Louisiana, Nebraska, New Jersey, Oregon, Pennsylvania, Utah, Virginia, and Wyoming), with another forty million citizens, have laws which in the Committee's opinion provide little or no effective protection. Thus, eighty million Americans, nearly 40% of our population, have no meaningful protection from debt collection abuse.

While thirty-seven States and the District of Columbia do have laws regulating Debt Collectors, only a small number have comprehensive statutes which provide a civil remedy. As an example of ineffective State laws, of the sixteen States which regulate by debt collection boards, twelve require by law that a majority of the board be comprised by Debt Collectors.

The Committee has found that collection abuse has grown from a State problem to a national problem. The use of WATS lines by Debt Collectors has led to a dramatic increase in interstate collections. State law enforcement officials have pointed to this development as a prime reason why Federal legislation is necessary, because State Officials are unable to act against unscrupulous Debt Collectors who harass Consumers from another State.

One of the most frequent fallacies concerning Debt Collection legislation is the contention that the primary beneficiaries are "deadbeats." In fact, however, there is universal agreement among scholars, law enforcement officials, and even Debt Collectors that the number of persons who willfully refuse to pay just debts is miniscule.

Prof. David Caplovitz, the foremost authority on Debtors in default, testified that after years of research he has found that only four percent of all defaulting Debtors fit the description of "deadbeat." This conclusion is supported by the National Commission of Consumer Finance which found that Creditors list the willful refusal to pay as an extremely infrequent reason for default.

The Commission's findings are echoed in all major studies: the vast majority of Consumers who obtain credit fully intend to repay their debts. When default occurs, it is nearly always due to an unforseen event such as unemployment, over-extension, serious illness, marital difficulties, or divorce.

The Committee believes that the serious and widespread abuses in this area and the inadequacy of existing State and Federal laws make this legislation necessary and appropriate.

Explanation Of The Legislation

This bill applies only to debts contracted by Consumers for personal, family, or household purposes; it has no application to the collection of commercial accounts.

The committee intends the term Debt Collector, subject to the exclusions discussed below, to cover all third persons who regularly collect debts for others. The primary persons intended to be covered are independent Debt Collectors. The requirement that debt collection be done "regularly" would exclude a person who collects a debt for another in an isolated instance, but would include those who collect for others in the regular course of business. The definition would include "reciprocal collections" whereby one Creditor regularly collects delinquent debts for another pursuant to a reciprocal service agreement, unless otherwise excluded by the act.

The term Debt Collector is not intended to include the following: "in house" collectors for Creditors so long as they use the Creditor's true business name when collecting; Government officials, such as Marshals and Sheriffs, while in the conduct of their official duties; process servers; nonprofit Consumer Credit Counseling Services which assist Consumers by apportioning the Consumer's income among his Creditors pursuant to a prior agreement; and Attorneys-at-law while acting in that capacity. One subsidiary or affiliate which collects debts for another subsidiary or affiliate is not a Debt Collector so long as the collecting affiliate collects only for other related entities and its principle business is not debt collection.

Finally, the Committee does not intend the definition to cover the activities of trust departments, escrow companies, or other bona fide loans, by persons who originated such loans; mortgage service companies and others who service outstanding debts for others, so long as the debts were not in default when taken for servicing; and the collection of debts owed to a Creditor when the Collector is holding the receivable account as collateral for commercial credit extended to the Creditor.

Obtaining Location Information

While this legislation strongly protects the Consumer's right to privacy by prohibiting a Debt Collector from communicating the Consumer's personal affairs to third persons, the Committee also recognizes the Debt Collector's legitimate need to seek the whereabouts of missing Debtors. Accordingly, this bill permits Debt Collectors to contact third persons for the purpose of obtaining the Consumer's location. In seeking this information, however, the Debt Collector must observe certain guidelines: he may not state that the Consumer owes a debt nor contact third persons more than once unless necessary to obtain complete information. In addition, a Debt Collector may not place language or symbols on mail to third persons indicating that the mail relates to debt collection nor continue to contact third parties after learning the name and address of the Consumer's Attorney, unless the Attorney fails to respond to the Debt Collector's communications.

Prohibited Practices

This legislation expressly prohibits a host of harassing, deceptive, and unfair Debt Collection practices. These include: threats of violence; obscene language; the publishing of "shame lists," harassing or anonymous telephone calls; impersonating a Government Official or Attorney; misrepresenting the Consumer's legal rights; simulating court process; obtaining information under false pretenses; collecting more than is legally owing; and misusing postdated checks. In addition to these specific prohibitions, this bill prohibits in general terms any harassing, unfair, or deceptive collection practice. This will enable the courts, where appropriate, to prescribe other improper conduct which is not specifically addressed.

In addition, this legislation adopts an extremely important protection recommended by the National Commission on Consumer Finance and already the law in fifteen States: it prohibits disclosing the Consumer's personal affairs to third persons. Other than to obtain location information, a Debt Collector may not contact third persons such as Consumer's friends, neighbors, relatives, or employer. Such contacts are not legitimate collection practices and result in serious invasions of privacy, as well as the loss of jobs.

Validation Of Debts

Another significant feature of this legislation is its provision requiring the validation of debts. After initially contacting a Consumer, a Debt Collector must send him or her written notice stating the name of the Creditor and the amount owed. If the Consumer disputes the validity of the debt within thirty days, the Debt Collector must cease collection until he sends the Consumer verification.

This provision will eliminate the recurring problem of Debt Collectors dunning the wrong person or attempting to collect debts which the Consumer has already paid. Since the current practice of most Debt Collectors is to send similar information to Consumers, this provision will not result in additional expense or paperwork.

Legal Actions By Debt Collectors

This legislation also addresses the problem of "forum abuse," an unfair practice in which Debt Collectors file suit against Consumers in Courts which are so distant or inconvenient that Consumers are unable to appear. As a result, the Debt Collector obtains a Default Judgement and the Consumer is denied his day in court.

In response to this practice, the bill adopts the Fair Venue Standards developed by the Federal Trade Commission. A Debt Collector who files suit must do so either where the Consumer resides or where the underlying contract was signed. When an action is against real property, it must be brought where such property is located.

More than 1,000 Collection Agencies in all fifty States have already voluntarily agreed to follow these standards. The Commission reports that this standard is effective in curtailing forum abuse without unreasonably restricting Debt Collectors.

Furnishing Deceptive Forms

Another common collection abuse is known colloquially as "flat-rating." A "flat-rater" is one who sells to Creditors a set of dunning letters bearing the letter-head of the flat-rater's Collection Agency and exhorting the Debtor to pay the Creditor at once. The Creditor sends these letters to his Debtors, giving the impression that a third party Debt Collector is collecting the debt. In fact, however, the flat-rater is not in the business of debt collection, but merely sells dunning letters.

This bill prohibits the practice of flat-rating because of its inherently deceptive nature. The prohibition on furnishing such forms does not apply, however, to printers and custom stationary sellers who innocently print or sell such forms without knowledge of their intended use.

Civil Liability

The committee views this legislation as primarily self-enforcing; Consumers who have been subjected to collection abuses will be enforcing compliance.

A Debt Collector who violates the act is liable for any actual damages he caused as well as any additional damages the court deems appropriate, not exceeding $1,000. In assessing damages, the Court must take into account the nature of the violation, the degree of willfullness, and the Debt Collector's persistence. A Debt Collector has no liability, however, if he violates the act in any manner, including with regard to the act's coverage, when such violation is unintentional and occurred despite procedures designed to avoid such violations. A Debt Collector also has no liability if he relied in good faith on an advisory opinion issued by the Federal Trade Commission. As in all other Federal Consumer Protection legislation, a

Consumer who obtains Judgement on his behalf is entitled to Attorney's fees and costs. In order to protect Debt Collectors from nuisance lawsuits, if the Court finds that an action was brought by a Consumer in bad faith and for harassment, the Court may award the Debt Collector reasonable Attorney's fees and costs.

Administrative Enforcement

This legislation is enforced administratively primarily by the Federal Trade Commission. If a depository institution subject to regulation by another Federal Agency engages in Debt Collection, administrative enforcement authority is lodged with that Agency.

All enforcement agencies are authorized to utilize all their functions and powers to enforce compliance. The Federal Trade Commission is authorized to treat violations of the act as violations of a trade regulation rule, which empowers the Commission to obtain restraining orders and seek fines in Federal District Court.

Because the Committee regards this act as comprehensive legislation which fully addresses the problem of collection abuses, the administrative agencies charged with enforcement are specifically prohibited from issuing additional rules or regulations applicable to persons covered by this legislation.

Relation To State Law

The Committee believes that this law ought not to foreclose the States from enacting or enforcing their own laws regarding debt collection. Accordingly, this legislation annuls only "inconsistent" State laws, with stronger State laws not regarded as inconsistent. In addition, States with substantially similar laws may be exempted from the act's requirements (but not its remedies) by applying to the Federal Trade Commission.

Cost Of This Legislation

Enactment of this legislation will result in no new additional costs to the Federal Government. The Congressional Budget Office analysis of this bill is contained in the following letter:

> Congressional Budget Office
> U.S. Congress
> Washington, D.C.
> July 27, 1977.

Hon. William Proxmire, Chairman,
Committee on Banking, Housing, and Urban Affairs
U.S. Senate, Washington, D.C.

Dear Mr. Chairman:

Pursuant to section 403 of the Congressional Budget Act of 1974, the Congressional Budget Office has reviewed H.R. 5294, a bill to amend the Consumer Credit Protection Act to prohibit abusive practices by Debt Collectors, as ordered reported by the Senate Committee on Banking, Housing, and Urban Affairs, July 26, 1977.

Based on this review, it appears that no additional cost to the Government would be incurred as a result of enactment of this bill.

> Sincerely,
> *Alice M. Rivlin*, Director

OBTAINED FROM:

2 U.S. Cong. & Admin. News 77-26
Senate Report # 95-382 Pages 1695-1701

Summary Of Legislation

Section-By-Section Summary of the FAIR DEBT COLLECTION PRACTICES ACT.

Section 801 SHORT TITLE—The act may be cited as the *Fair Debt Collection Practices Act.*

Section 802 FINDINGS AND PURPOSE—The Congress finds that collection abuses by independent Debt Collectors are serious and widespread and that existing State laws are inadequate to curb these abuses. The purpose of the title is to eliminate abusive practices, not disadvantage ethical Debt Collectors, and promote consistent state action.

Section 803 DEFINITIONS—The term "Debt Collector" is defined to include all third parties who regularly collect Consumer debts for others, except for the following persons: "in house" Collection Creditors; affiliates collecting for one another, providing that collection is not the principle business of the affiliate; Government Officials collecting in their official capacities; process servers; bona fide Consumer Credit Counseling Services; and Attorneys-at-law. The term also does not include trust companies and other bona fide fiduciaries; persons collecting loans which they originated; persons who service debts for others; and persons holding receivables as collateral for commercial credit transactions.

Section 804 ACQUISITION OF LOCATION INFOR-
MATION—When contacting third persons to establish
a Consumer's whereabouts, a Debt Collector may not:
state that the Consumer owes a debt; contact the third
person more than once unless reasonably necessary;
or use language symbols on mail indicating that it
pertains to debt collection. A Debt Collector may not
contact a third person if the Debt Collector knows
that the Consumer is represented by an Attorney and
has the Attorney's name and address.

Section 805 COMMUNICATION IN CONNECTION
WITH DEBT COLLECTION—Without the Consumer's consent, a Debt Collector may not (A) contact
a Consumer at any unusual or inconvenient time or
place (8 A.M. to 9 P.M. is considered convenient);
(B) contact a Consumer if he is represented by an
Attorney; or (C) call a Consumer at work if the Debt
Collector knows the Consumer's employer prohibits
such calls.

There is a general prohibition on contacting any
third parties (other than to obtain location information)
except for: the Consumer's Attorney; a Credit
Reporting Agency; the Creditor; the Creditor's or Debt
Collector's Attorney; or any other person to the extent
necessary to effectuate a post-Judgement judicial
remedy.

If a Consumer notifies a Debt Collector in writing
that he refuses to pay a debt or wishes the Debt
Collector to cease further contacts, the Debt Collector
must cease communications except to notify the
Consumer of the Debt Collector's or Creditor's
possible further actions.

Section 806 HARASSMENT OR ABUSE—A Debt Collector is prohibited from engaging in any conduct the natural consequences of which is to harass, oppress or abuse any person. The following enumerated practices are violations: threats of violence; use of profane or obscene language; publishing "shame lists;" repeated telephone calls intended to annoy or harass; and making telephone calls without disclosing the caller's identity.

Section 807 FALSE OR MISLEADING REPRESEN-TATIONS—A debt Collector is prohibited from using any false, deceptive or misleading representations to collect debts. The following enumerated practices are violations: misrepresenting that a Debt Collector is a Goverment official; misrepresenting the amount or nature of a debt; impersonating an Attorney; misrepresenting that a Consumer will be arrested or his property seized; misrepresenting a Consumer's legal rights; deliberately communicating false credit information; utilizing bogus legal documents; and misrepresenting a Collection Agency as a Credit Bureau.

Section 808 UNFAIR PRACTICES—A Debt Collector is prohibited from using any unfair or unconscionable means to collect debts. The following enumerated practices are violations: collecting amounts in excess of the debt or interest owed; causing charges for communications to be billed to a Consumer; repossessing property if there is no valid security interest or if it is exempt by law from repossession; communicating information about a debt by postcard; and using symbols on envelopes indicating that the contents pertain to debt collection.

Section 809 VALIDATION OF DEBTS—Within 5 days after contacting a Consumer, the Debt Collector must in writing notify the Consumer of the amount of the debt and the name of the Creditor and advise the Consumer of the Debt Collector's duty to verify the debt if it is disputed. If a Consumer disputes a debt within 30 days, the Debt Collector must stop collection until verification is sent to the Consumer.

Section 810 MULTIPLE DEBTS—A Debt Collector is prohibited from applying payments to disputed debts and, where applicable, must apply payments in accordance with the Consumer's directions.

Section 811 LEGAL ACTIONS BY DEBT COLLEC-TORS—Actions on real property are required to be brought in the judicial district in which the property is located. In personal action, suits must be brought either where the contract was signed or where the Consumer resides.

Secion 812 FURNISHING CERTAIN DECEPTIVE FORMS—It is made unlawful to compile, design, and furnish forms knowing that they will be used to create the false impression that a third person is collecting a debt.

Section 813 CIVIL LIABILITY—A Debt Collector who violates the act is liable for actual damages plus costs and reasonable Attorney's fees. The Court may award additional damages of up to $1,000 in individual actions, and in class actions, up to $500,000 or 1% of the Debt Collector's net worth, whichever is less.

Two defenses are provided: good faith reliance or a FAIR TRADE COMMISSION advisory opinion; and bona fide error notwithstanding procedures to avoid the error. Where a Court finds that a suit was brought by a Consumer in bad faith and for harassment, the court may award reasonable Attorney's fees to the defendant.

Jurisdiction for actions is conferred on U.S. District and State Court; there is a 1 year statute of limitations.

Section 814 ADMINISTRATIVE ENFORCEMENT— The Act is administratively enforced by the FEDERAL TRADE COMMISSION and the Federal Bank Regulatory Agencies. The agencies are empowered to use all their functions and powers to enforce compliance. The agencies are prohibited from promulgating any additional rules or regulations pertaining to Debt Collectors.

Section 815 REPORTS TO CONGRESS BY THE COMMISSION—The Federal Trade Commission shall provide annual reports to Congress on the Act's effectiveness and administrative enforcement.

Section 816 RELATION TO STATE LAW—The Act annuls State laws only if inconsistent; a State law is not inconsistent if it provides greater protection than this title.

Section 817 EXEMPTION FOR STATE REGULATION—The Federal Trade Commission may exempt from the Act any collection practices within any State if subject to substantially similar requirements.

Section 818 EFFECTIVE DATE—The Act is effective 6 months from enactment.

Individual State Laws

Many State Laws provide additional protection for the Consumer that sometimes override Federal Law as stated in the *Fair Debt Collection Practices Act*. Unfortunately, not all States provide additional protection. They rely solely on the FDCPA with a belief that this law provides all the protection the Consumer needs.

In the following pages, I have listed a few States that *do* provide additional protection. This list is not, by any means, a complete guide to State Collection Laws, but a select few regulations that should interest you. The reason this list is not complete is because the majority of the laws from each State duplicate the laws in the FDCPA. Only those laws which provide *additional, unique* (not covered under the FDCPA), or a more *strict* application of a similar law are shown.

For a *complete* copy of the laws in your State, contact your local library.

Arizona

R4-4-1512

> A Collection Agency shall not contact a Debtor at his place of employment unless a reasonable attempt has been made to first contact the Debtor at his place of residence, and such attempt has failed.

R4-4-1513A

A Collection Agency shall cease all contacts, direct or indirect, with the Debtor if and when the Debtor informs the Collection Agency that he is represented by an Attorney and further communications relative to the debt should be directed to said Attorney. (Unless the Collection Agency discovers that no bona fide Attorney/Client relationship exists.)

R4-4-1514

A Collection Agency must disclose to the Debtor from whom it is attempting to collect the debt in the name of the Creditor, the time and place of the creation of the debt, the merchandise, services or other things of value underlying the debt, and the date when the account was turned over to the Collection Agency by the Creditor.

R4-4-1520B

Before using a name other than his true name while engaged in the collection of a claim, a licensee shall set forth in a separate record of the Agency the following:

    a.   True name of Debt Collector;

    b.   Name used other than true name and inclusive dates the name is used;

    c.   True physical home address and true mailing address;

    d.   A copy of the record of fictitious names shall be filed with the State banking department on a semi-annual basis on July 1 and December 31 of each year. After the initial report is filed, only changes need be reported to the department.

California

California Consumer Affairs Act

Sec. 625.5

> Within 60 days after an overpayment of one dollar or more on any claim is received from a Debtor or it has been determined that a refund of one dollar or more is due a Debtor on any claim that has been made, the licensee shall account for and remit to the Debtor the money due him. The money shall be paid from the licensee's trust account. Money due a Debtor for an obligation or a credit on a debt may not be offset against any other obligation owed by the Debtor unless the Debtor has so authorized in writing.

California Business and Professional Code

Sec. 6927(a)

> A collection Agency shall notify a Debtor in writing that a Debtor's debt has been cancelled by the Collection Agency and returned to the Creditor when the Debtor has requested verification of the debt and the Collection Agency has not been able to provide the Debtor with such verification or when the Debtor has contested the validity of the debt and, as a result has cancelled the debt back to the Creditor.

Sec. 6927(b)

> The Collection Agency shall not be subject to the notification requirements of subdivision (a) only if the Debtor has notified the Collection Agency of the Debtor's address.

Sec. 6947(h)

> No licensee or employee shall: Use any name while engaged in the collection of claims, other than his true

name, except under conditions prescribed by rules and regulations adopted by the Director.

California Administrative Code, Rules and Regulations,

Sec. 630—Use of name other than true name

Any person using an alias in the collection of claims for a licensee shall register such alias with the licensee and with the Bureau. No person may have more than one alias and no alias may be used by more than one person. Such alias shall be the property of the individual. No change of alias shall be allowed unless good cause is shown.

Civil Code

Sec. 1788.14

No Debt Collector shall collect or attempt to collect any consumer debt by means of the following practices:

(b)   Collecting or attempting to collect from the Debtor the whole or any part of the Debt Collector's fee or charge for services rendered, or other expense incurred by the Debt Collector in the collection of the Consumer debt, except as permitted by law.

California Administrative Code, Rules and Regulations,

Sec. 620—Written Communications.

(a)   Any written communication sent in demand of money to a Debtor shall set forth on its face in clear and legible type the name by which the licensee is authorized to do business and its telephone number and address of record.

(c)   The name of the Creditor and the amount due shall be clearly designated on any initial notice to a Debtor. If the amount of the demand is thereafter increased for any reason, including the addition of interest, the next succeeding notice to such Debtor shall separately identify the amount and nature of the additional claim, and identify the additional Creditor, if any.

(e) Any such written communication when used shall bear the specific date the licensee mailed the form to the Debtor.

California Administrative Code, Rules and Regulations,

Sec.627(c)

The envelope or container of any written communication addressed to a Debtor at his or her place of employment shall be clearly marked PERSONAL AND CONFIDENTIAL outside and immediately adjacent to the name and address of the Debtor, and shall be printed in upper-case, large, bold-face letters. No envelope or container many show the name of the Collections Agency or include any reference to an alleged debt.

Civil Code

Sec. 1788.16

It is unlawful, with respect to attempted collection of a Consumer debt, for a Debt Collector, Creditor or an Attorney, to send a communication which simulates legal or judicial process or which gives the appearance of being authorized, issued, or approved by a Governmental Agency or Attorney when it is not. Any violation of the provisions of this section is a misdemeanor punishable by imprisonment in the county jail not exceeding six months, or by a fine not exceeding $2,500 or by both.

Colorado

Article 14, Title 12 Colorado Revised Statutes

Sec. 104—Location information

(f)   After the Debt Collector or Collection Agency knows the Consumer is represented by an Attorney with regard to the subject debt and has knowledge of, or can readily ascertain, such Attorney's name and address he shall not communicate with any person other than that Attorney, unless the Attorney fails to respond within a reasonable period of time (not less than 30 days) to communication from the Debt Collector or Collection Agency.

12-114-105(3) (a)

If a Consumer notifies a Debt Collector or Collection Agency in writing that:

(1)   The Consumer wishes the Collection Agency to cease contact by telphone at the Consumer's place of employment, then no such further contact by telephone shall be made;

(2)   The Consumer refuses to pay a debt or the Consumer wishes the Collection Agency to cease further communication with the Consumer, then the Debt Collector or Collection Agency shall not communicate further with the Consumer with respect to such debt, except:

(A)   To advise the Consumer that the Collection Agency's further efforts are being terminated;

(B)   To notify the Consumer that the Collection Agency or Creditor may invoke such specific remedies which are ordinarily invoked by said Collection Agency or Creditor; or

(C)   Where applicable to notify the Consumer that the Collection Agency or Creditor intends to invoke a specified remedy permitted by law.

    (b)   If such notice from the Consumer is made by mail, notification shall be complete upon receipt.

    (c)   With the initial written communication to the Consumer, the Collection Agency shall notify the Consumer in writing of the Consumer's rights under the subsection (3).

Georgia

Georgia Statutes

Sec. 120-1-14-.23—Fradulent, Deceptive or Misleading Representations

No Debt Collector shall use any fraudulent, deceptive or misleading representation or means to collect or attempt to collect claims or to obtain information concerning a Consumer or Consumers. Without limiting the general application of the foregoing, the following conduct will be deemed to violate this section:

(1)   The use of any name, while engaged in debt collection, other that the Debt Collector's true name;

(4)   The failure to clearly disclose the name and full business address of the person to whom the claim

has been assigned for collection, or to whom the claim is owed, at the time of making any demand for money.

Hawaii

Chapter 443A, Hawaii Revised Statutes

Sec. 443A-15—Fraudulent. Deceptive, or Misleading Representations

No Collection Agency shall use any fraudulent, deceptive, or misleading repesentation or means to collect, or attempt to collect, claims or to obtain information concerning a Debtor or alleged Debtor, including any conduct which is described as follows:

(4)   The failure to clearly disclose the name and full business address of the person to whom the claim has been assigned for collection or to whom the claim is owed at the time of making any demand for money.

Sec. 443A.16—Unfair or Unconscionable Means

No Collection Agency shall use unfair or unscons-cionable means to collect or attempt to collect any claim in any of the following ways:

(3)   The collection or the attempt to collect from a Debtor or alleged Debtor all or any part of the Collection Agency's fees or charges for services rendered.

Illinois

Rules and Regulations Promulgated for the Administration of the Collection Agency Act

Rule 7—Use of Pseudonyms.

If any person employed by an Agency uses a pseudonym, such Agency shall provide the department with a list of the respective pseudonyms used and the correct identity of each individual using a pseudonym. When there has been a change in personnel or a pseudonym or additions to either, such Agency shall file a list of the changes and additions, or either, as the case may be, within 30 days after such change or addition.

Massachusetts

209CMR: Division of Banks and Loan Agencies

Sec. 18.13: Forms and Identification of a Collection Agency

An envelope sent through the mails to a Consumer Debtor by a Collection Agency engaged in the collection of retail accounts against Consumer Debtors shall not contain as part of a return address the name of the Collection Agency or any signification that the communication is related to a debt allegedly overdue. A communication in an envelope to a Debtor by a Collection Agency shall disclose the business address of the Agency. A Collection Agency engaged in the collection of retail accounts against Consumer Debtors shall disclose its telephone number and office hours on all communication to the Consumer Debtor. In communicating with Debtors the Collection Agency shall use only the exact name in which the Commissioner has granted the license.

18.15: Contact With Debtors

(1) It shall constitute an unfair or deceptive act or

practice for a Collection Agency to contact a Debtor in any of the following ways:

(b) Threatening that nonpayment of a debt will result in:

2. Granishment of any wages of any Debtor or the taking of other action requiring a judicial order without informing the Debtor that there must be in effect a judicial order permitting such garnishment or such other action before it can be taken;

(d) Communicating by telephone without disclosure of the name of the Collection Agency and without disclosure of the personal name of the individual making such communication provided, however, that any individual utilizing a personal name other than his own shall use only one such personal name at all times and provided that a mechanism is established by the Collection Agency to identify the person using such personal name; the Collection Agency shall submit a list of all such personal names and the person using same to the Commissioner.

(f) Engaging any Debtor in communication via telephone, initiated by the Collection Agency, in excess of two calls in each seven-day period at a Debtor's residence and two calls in each 30-day period other than at a Debtor's residence, for each debt, provided that for the purpose of this division, a Creditor may treat any billing address of the Debtor as his place of residence;

(h) Placing any telephone calls to the Debtor's place of employment if the Debtor has made a written or oral request that such telephone calls not be made at the place of employment, provided, that any oral request shall be valid for only 10 days unless the Debtor provides written confirmation postmarked or delivered within seven days of such request. A Debtor may at any time terminate such a request by written communication to the Collection Agency;

NOTICE OF IMPORTANT RIGHTS

You have the right to make a written or oral request that telephone calls regarding your debt not be made to you at your place of employment. Any such oral request will be valid for only 10 days unless you provide written confirmation of the request postmarked or delivered within seven days of such request. You may terminate this request by writing to the Collection Agency.

(j) Visiting the household of a Debtor at times other than the normal waking hours of such Debtor, or if normal waking hours are not known, at any time other than between 8 A.M. and 9 P.M., provided however that in no event shall such visits, initiated by the Collection Agency, exceed one in any 30-day period for each debt, excluding visits where no person is contacted in the household, unless the Debtor consents in writing to more frequent visits, provided, further, that at all times the Creditor must remain outside the household unless expressly invited inside by such Debtor; and provided further, that visits to the household of a Debtor which are solely for the propose of repossessing any collateral or propety of the Creditor (including but not limited to credit cards, drafts, notes or the like), are not limited under this division;

(k)   Visiting the place of employment of a Debtor, unless requested by the Debtor excluding visits which are solely for the purpose of repossessing any collateral or property of the Creditor, or confrontations with the Debtor regarding the collection of a debt initiated by a Collection Agency in a public place excluding court houses, the Collection Agency's place of business, other place agreed to by a Debtor, or places where the conversation between persons representing the Collection Agency and a Debtor cannot be reasonably overheard by any other person not authorized by the Debtor;

Sec. 18.17:

Contact with persons other than Consumer Debtors or Debtor may be made only if Collection Agency does not have correct information as to the Debtor's current residence or location and provided further, that the Collection Agency reasonably believes that the earlier response of such person, if any, is erroneous or incomplete and that such person now has correct or complete locational information, and in no event shall such contacts exceed three per person contacted in any 12-month period for each debt. The Collection Agency in making said contacts may reveal only his personal name unless the recipient expressly requests the disclosure of the company name provided, however, that any such individual using a personal name other than his own shall use only one such personal name at all times and provided that a mechanism is established by such Collection Agency to identify the person using such personal name.

Sec. 18.19: Disclosure

(1) It shall constitute an unfair or deceptive act or practice for a Collection Agency to omit to disclose to a Debtor in writing, by delivering or mailing, within five days after the first contact by the Collection Agency with a Debtor, the following information if such first contact is made after the effective date of these regulations:

(a) The name and mailing address of the Collection Agency and proper identification of the creditor or the assignee of the Creditor on whose behalf the Collection Agency is communicating;

(b) Identification of the debt;

(c) A brief description of the nature of the default;

(e) The name, address and telephone number of the person to be contacted for additional information concerning the debt and default;

Sec. 18.21: Postdated Checks

It shall be an unfair or deceptive act or practice for a Collection Agency to request or demand from a Debtor a postdated check, draft, order for withdrawal or other similar instrument in payment for the debt or any portion thereof, or for a Collection Agency to negotiate such instrument before the due date of the instrument.

Michigan

Occupational Code, Act 299 of 1980,

Article 9, Sec. 339.915— Licensee, Prohibited Acts

   (h)   Communicating with the Debtor, except through billing procedure, when the Debtor is actively represented by an Attorney, the Attorney's name and address are known, and the Attorney has been contacted in writing by the credit grantor or the credit grantor's representative or agent, unless the Attorney representing the Debtor fails to answer written communication or fails to discuss the claim on its merits within 30 days after receipt of the written communication.

   (i)   Communicating information relating to a Debtor's indebtedness to an employer or an employer's agent unless the communication is specifically authorized in writing by the Debtor subsequent to the forwarding of the claim for collection, the communication is in response to an inquiry initiated by the Debtor's employer or the employer's agent, or the communication is for the purpose of acquiring location information about the Debtor.

   (j)   Using or employing, in connection with collection of a claim, a person acting as a peace or law enforcement officer or any other officer authorized to serve legal papers.

Sec. 915(a)—A licensee shall not commit one or more of the following acts:

   (a)   Listing the name of an Attorney in a written or oral communication, collection letter, or publication.

(o) Permitting an employee to use a name other than the employee's own name or the assumed name registered by the licensee with the department in the collection of a debt.

New Hampshire

Laws 1975, Chapter 437

Sec. 358-C: 3—Prohibited Acts.

For the purposes of this chapter, any debt collection or attempt to collect a debt shall be deemed unfair, deceptive, or unreasonable if the Debt Collector:

1. Communicates or attempts to communicate with a Debtor, orally or in writing:

    (c) At the Debtor's place of employment if said place is other than the Debtor's residence provided that:

        (1) A Debt Collector may send a single letter to the Debtor at his place of employment if he has otherwise been unable to locate the Debtor; and

        (2) A Debt Collector may phone the Debtor at his place of employment if he is unable to contact the Debtor at his residence, provided that:

            A. The Debtor does not inform the Debt Collector that he does not wish the Debt Collector to communicate or attempt to communicate with him at his place of employment; and

B.   The Debt Collector shall not inform the employer of the nature of the call unless asked by the employer; and

C.   In no event shall the Debt Collector make more than one phone call per month to the Debtor at his place of employment unless the Debtor affirmatively indicates in writing that he desires the Debt Collector to call him at his place of employment. (For the purpose of this subparagraph, any language in any instrument creating the debt which purports to authorize phone calls at the Debtor's place of employment shall not be considered an affirmative indication that the Debtor desires the Debt Collector to call him at his place of employment.); or

D.   Using any written communication which fails to clearly identify the name of the Debt Collector, the name of the person for whom the Debt Collector is attempting to collect the debt, and the Debt Collector's business address, or

E.   By placement of phone calls without disclosure of the name of the individual making the call and the name of the person for whom the Debt Collector is attempting to collect the debt, or by using a fictitious name while engaging in the collection of debts.

2. Communicates directly with the Debtor, except through proper legal action, after notification from an Attorney, financial counseling organization, or other person representing the Debtor that all further communication relative to the debt should be addressed to the Attorney, organization or other person unless the Attorney, organization, or other person fails to answer correspondence, return phone calls, or discuss the debt within 10 days or prior approval is obtained from the Attorney, organization, or other person or the communication is a response in the ordinary course of business to the Debtor's inquiry.

New Mexico

Department of Banking, Collection Agency Division, Rules, Pursuant to Sec. 67-15-29, NMSA, 1953 Compilation.

Rule 77-5A.

The use of fictitous names by any licensee or employee thereof or signatures by any licensee or employee thereof must be registered with and approved by the chief prior to their implementation.

North Carolina

Article 9, Chapter 6, General Statutes, Part 3

Sec. 66-43.4—Deceptive Representation

No Collection Agency shall collect or attempt to collect a debt or obtain information concerning a Consumer by any fraudulent, deceptive or misleading representation. Such representations include, but are not limited to the following:

(1) Communicating with the Consumer other than in the name of the person making the communication, the Collection Agency and the person or business on whose behalf the Collection Agency is acting, or to whom the debt is owed.

Sec. 66-43.7—Shared Office Space

The office of a Collection Agency shall not be shared or have a common waiting room with a practicing Attorney or any type of lending institution. The office may be located in a private residence only if it is solely for business purposes, has an outside entrance and can be isolated from the remainder of the residence.

North Dakota

Chapter 13-04-02, Collection Agencies

Sec. 13-04-02-08

No Debt Collector shall use any fraudulent, deceptive or misleading representation or means to collect or attempt to collect claims or to obtain information concerning Consumers. Without limiting the general application of the foregoing, the following conduct is deemed to violate this section:

1. The use of any name while engaged in the collection of claims other than the Debt Collector's true name.

4. The failure to clearly disclose the name and full business address of the person to whom the claim has been assigned or is owed at the time of making any demand for money.

Oregon

ORS 646,639

(2)   It shall be an unlawful collection practice for a Debt Collector, while collecting or attempting to collect a debt to do any of the following:

(c)   Threaten the seizure, attachment, or sale of a Debtor's property where such action can only be taken pursuant to a court order without disclosing that prior court proceedings are required.

(g)   Communicate without the Debtor's permission or threaten to communicate with the Debtor at the Debtor's place of employment or such places other than the Debtor's residence, except that the Debt Collector may:

(A)   Write to the Debtor at the Debtor's place of employment if no home address is reasonably available and if the envelope does not reveal that the communication is from a Debt Collector other than a provider of the goods or services from which the debt arose.

(B)   Telephone a Debtor's place of employment without informing any other person of the nature of the call or identifying the caller as a Debt Collector, but only if the Debt Collector is unable to contact a Debtor at the Debtor's residence. The Debt Collector may not contact the Debtor at the Debtor's place of employment more frequently than once each business week.

(i)   Communicate with the Debtor verbally without disclosing to the Debtor within 30 seconds the name of the individual making the contact and the true purpose thereof.

Pennsylvania

Part V. Bureau of Consumer Protection, 37 PA Code, Chapter 303—Debt Collection Trade Practices

Sec. 303.4—Communications and Contacts with the Debtor.

While engaged in the collection of debts it shall be an unfair or deceptive act or practice for a creditor or a Debt Collector to engage in any of the following acts or practices:

(2)   Abusing or harassing the Debtor by telephone. For the purpose of this section a rebuttable presumption of abuse or harassment shall be created if a Creditor or Debt Collector continues to telephone the Debtor during any seven-day period following a telephone discussion between a Creditor or Debt Collector and the Debtor. Evidence of reasonable follow-up activity may be sufficient to rebut the presumption of abuse or harassment. However, in no event shall the Creditor or Debt Collector place telephone calls to the Debtor at the Debtor's place of employment, which is not the current billing address of the account, unless:

(i)   The Creditor or Debt Collector has been unable to effect a discussion regarding the debt with the Debtor during the preceding 30-day period by telephone calls or personal visits; and

(ii) The Creditor or Debt Collector does not know or has no reason to know that the Debtor's employer prohibits such contacts.

(4) Abusing or harassing the Debtor by household visits. For the purpose of this paragraph, a rebuttable presumption of abuse or harassment shall be created if the Creditor or Debt Collector continues to visit the household of the Debtor during any 30-day period following a visit which resulted in a discussion between the Creditor or Debt Collector and the Debtor. Evidence of reasonable follow-up activity may be sufficient to rebut the presumption of abuse or harassment.

(5) Entering the household of a Debtor unless expressly invited inside by the Debtor or any adult person in the household of the Debtor.

(6) Failing to leave the Debtor's premises when asked to do so by the Debtor or by any person in the household of the Debtor.

(7) Mailing communications to the Debtor at the Debtor's place of employment, unless the current billing address of the account is the Debtor's place of employment or unless the Debtor specifically consents to such communications in writing subsequent to the commencement of collection activities.

(8) Visiting the Debtor at the Debtor's place of employment, unless in response to a written request from the Debtor.

Texas

Article 5069, Chapter 11

Sec.5—Unfair or Unconscionable Means.

(e) Using any written communication which fails to clearly indicate the name of the Debt Collector and the Debt Collector's street address, when the written notice refers to an alleged delinquent debt;

(f) Using any written communication which demands a response to a place other than the Debt Collector's or Creditor's street address or post office box.

Washington

Chapter 19.16RCW—Collection Agencies

Sec. 19.16.250—Prohibited Practices.

No licensee or employee of a licensee shall;

(8) Give or send to any Debtor or cause to be given or sent to any Debtor, any notice, letter, message, or form which represents or implies that a claim exists unless it shall indicate in clear and legible type:

(a) The name of the licensee and the city, street, and number at which he is licensed to do business;

(b) The name of the original Creditor to whom the Debtor owed the claim if such name is known to the licensee or employee; provided, that upon written request of the Debtor, the licensee shall make a reasonable effort to obtain the name of such a person and provide this name to the Debtor;

(c) If the notice, letter, message, or form is the first notice to the Debtor or if the licensee is attempting to collect a different amount than indicated on his or its first notice to the Debtor, an itemization of the claim asserted must be made including:

   (i) amount owing on the original obligation at the time it was received by the licensee for collection or by assignment;

   (ii) interest or service charge, collection cost, or late payment charges, if any, added to the original obligation by the original Creditor, customer, or assignor before it was received by the licensee for collection, if such information is known by the licensee or employee; provided, that upon written request of the Debtor, the licensee shall make a reasonable effort to obtain information on such items and provide this information to the Debtor;

   (iii) interest or service charge, if any, added by the licensee or customer or assignor after the obligation was received by the licensee for collection;

   (iv) collection costs, if any, that the licensee is attempting to collect;

   (v) Attorney's fees, if any, that the licensee is attempting to collect on his or its behalf or on the behalf of a customer or assignor.

   (vi) any other charge or fee that the licensee is attempting to collect on his or its own behalf or on the behalf of a customer or assignor.

(12) Communicate with the Debtor or anyone else in such a manner as to harass, intimidate, threaten, or embarrass the Debtor, including but not limited to communication at an unreasonable hour, with unreasonable frequency, by threats of force or violence, by threats of criminal prosecution and by use of offensive language. A communication shall be presumed to have been made for the purpose of harassment if:

(a)   It is made with the Debtor or spouse in any form, manner, or place, more than three times in a single week;

(b)   If it is made with the Debtor at his or her place of employment more than one time in a single week;

West Virginia

Article 16—Collection Agencies

Sec. 46A-2-127

No Debt Collector shall use any fraudulent, deceptive, or misleading representation or means to collect or attempt to collect claims or to obtain information concerning Consumers. Without limiting the general application of the foregoing, the following conduct is deemed to violate this section:

(d)   The failure to clearly disclose the name and full business address of the person to whom the claim has been assigned for collection, or to whom the claim is owed, at the time of making any demand for money.

Wisconsin

Chapter BKG74.12—Collection Agencies

Fair Collection Practice Notice.

> In oral or written communication with the Debtor, Collectors shall identify themselves by their birth given surname, their married name or a surname composed of their birth given name and married names. An alias or pseudonym may not be used. They shall also identify the Agency which they represent by the name in which it is licensed to do business. A licensee may not forward printed collection notices to a Debtor which are unsigned.

BKG74.14

> A licensee shall not engage in any oppressive or deceptive practices. In attempting to collect an alleged debt, a licensee shall not:

> (15) Enlist the aid of a neighbor or other third party to request that the Debtor contact the licensee except a person who resides with the Debtor or a third party with whom the Debtor has authorized the licensee to place such requests. This subsection shall not apply to a call-back message left at the Debtor's place of employment which is limited to the licensee's telephone number and the Collector's name.

Index

Abusive Language	22, 47, 73, 155
Adding Expenses	87
Answering Machines	41
Arrest	61
Attorney	48, 56
Bankruptcy	112, 123
Billing Errors	107
Calling at Work	17, 26, 58
Cease Communication	61
Consumer	26
Consumer Credit Counseling Services	104
Credit Application	118
Credit Bureau Reports	46, 120
Credit Cards	106
Credit Cards—Unauthorized Use	106
Creditor	26
Debt	26
Deceptive Letters	29
Disputes	49, 107
Divorce	102
Emergency	20, 58
Fair Debt Collection Practices Act	141
Fraud	68, 108

Garnishment   49, 69, 99
Hang-Ups   23, 60
Harassment   20, 35, 71, 155
Hours of Calling   36
Identification of Collector   21, 53
Interest   28
Judgement   98
Lawsuit   63, 94, 134, 148
Letters   44, 53
Lies   17, 64, 67
Non-Published Telephone Numbers   35
Overnight Mail   90
Paid In Full   93
Payments   78
P.O. Boxes   34
Postdated Checks   22, 91
Privacy   38
Purchased Accounts   103
Settlement   83
Social Security Reports   131
State Laws—   143, 159
   Arizona   159
   California   161
   Colorado   164
   Georgia   165
   Hawaii   166
   Illinois   166
   Massachusetts   167

Michigan	172
New Hampshire	173
New Mexico	175
North Carolina	176
North Dakota	177
Oregon	177
Pennsylvania	178
Texas	180
Washington	180
West Virginia	182
Wisconsin	183
Stop Payment	91
Student Loan	28
Third Party Disclosure	40, 48, 55
Threats	65, 66
Time Zones	39
Time Zone Map	40

Sources

Budish, Armond D. and Kurt Karakul, *Bankruptcy Can Save Your Home*, American Collectors Association

Consumer Credit Counseling Services and the Metro Denver Credit Association Company

Trans Union Credit Information Company

Weltman, Leslie Talbot, *Paid In Full*, Weinberg & Associates

Fair Debt Collection Practices Act 1977, Senate report Number 95-382, Section 801-818 public law of the FDCPA

2 U. S. Congress and Administration news 77-26

Senate Report #95-382 Pages 1695-1701

Books by Starburst Publishers

Like A Bulging Wall —Robert Borrud

Will you survive the 1990's economic crash? This book shows how debt, greed, and covetousness, along with a lifestyle beyond our means, has brought about an explosive situation in this country. Gives "call" from God to prepare for judgement in America, Also Lists TOP-RATED U.S. BANKS and SAVINGS & LOANS.

(trade paper) ISBN 0914984284 **$8.95**

What To Do When The Bill Collector Calls!
Know Your Rights —David L. Kelcher, Jr.

Reveals the unfair debt collection practices that some agencies use and how this has led to the invasion of privacy, bankruptcy, marital instability, and the loss of jobs. The reader is told what he can do about the problem.

(trade paper) ISBN 0914984322 **$9.95**

The Quick Job Hunt Guide —Robert D. Siedle

Gives techniques to use when looking for a job. Networking, Following the Ten-Day Plan, and Avoiding the Personnel Department, are some of the ways to "land that job!"

(trade paper) ISBN 0914984330 **$7.95**

Man And Wife For Life —Joseph Kanzlemar, Ed.D.

A penetrating and often humorous look into real life situations of married people. Helps the reader get a new understanding of the problems and relationships within marriage.

(trade paper) ISBN 0914984233 **$7.95**

Inch by Inch . . . Is It a Cinch? —Phyllis Miller

Is it a cinch to lose weight? If your answer is "NO," you must read this book. Read about the intimate details of one woman's struggle for love and acceptance.

(trade paper) ISBN 0914984152 **$8.95**

Purchasing Information

Listed books are available from your favorite Bookstore, either from current stock or special order. You may also order direct from STARBURST PUBLISHERS. When ordering enclose full payment plus $2.00* for shipping and handling ($2.50* if Canada or Overseas). Payment in US Funds only. Please allow two to three weeks minimum (longer overseas) for delivery. Make checks payable to and mail to STARBURST PUBLISHERS, P.O. Box 4123, LANCASTER, PA 17604. **Prices subject to change without notice**. Catalog available upon request.

* We reserve the right to ship your order the least expensive way. If you desire first class (domestic) or air shipment (overseas) please enclose shipping funds as follows: First Class within the USA enclose $4.00, Airmail Canada enclose $5.00, and Overseas enclose 30% (minimum $5.00) of total order. All remittance must be in US Funds.   07-91